Creative Self-Promotion on a Limited Budget

Creative Self-Promotion on a Limited Budget

by Sally Prince Davis

NORTH
LIGHT
BOOKS

Cincinnati, Ohio

96 95 94 93 92   5 4 3 2 1

Library of Congress Cataloging in Publication Data

Davis, Sally Prince
    Creative self-promotion on a limited budget / Sally Prince Davis — 1st ed.
        p.   cm.
    Includes index.
    ISBN 0-89134-438-1 (paper)
    1. Graphic arts — United States — Marketing. 2. Commercial art — United States — Marketing. I. Title.
NC1001.6.D37   1992
741.6′068′8 — dc20   92-9531
                                                                            CIP

Concept and editing by Diana Martin
Designed by Paul Neff

Dedication

This book is dedicated to Karen Prince Danner, Mary Louise Rowe and Jane Dalglish, three women whose unique gifts of the spirit will eternally inhabit this earth.

Acknowledgments

First and foremost, a heartfelt thank you to all of the graphic designers and illustrators included in this book, who so willingly gave of their time and promotional materials to make this project possible. For some it meant going "above and beyond" as phone calls were returned, materials sent by mail and courier, and special accommodations made to meet publishing needs. Next, a grateful acknowledgment and thank you to editors Diana Martin, Julie Whaley, and Mary Junewick, who kept *me* on track with cheerful encouragement and the *book* on track with skill and insight. Last, but certainly not least, a special thank you to Fran Aragon for faithful and prompt transcription of seemingly endless tapes, and to my family for their support and unfailing confidence.

About the Author

Sally Prince Davis is the author of *The Graphic Artist's Guide to Marketing and Self-promotion* and *The Fine Artist's Guide to Showing and Selling Your Work*. She is also a contributing editor to *The Artist's Magazine* and a former editor of *Artist's Market*, a yearly directory of freelance art markets.

Introduction

Self-promotion is important at any time in the life of a business; indeed, it is the lifeblood of a business. During times when budgetary belts tighten, businesspeople look for ways to keep their profiles high and the costs of their self-promotion low. This book is full of techniques and methods used by others in the same business who have met this problem head on and arrived at cost-effective and successful solutions.

If this book is any indicator, there is a trend away from glossy, high-cost, full-color promo pieces, and a movement toward self-promotion with a concept—something more than "just another pretty piece." I believe this is an extremely healthy sign, an indication that design itself is reaching a welcomed level. More and more the goal is not to design a piece and then "settle" for one-color printing, but rather to start with the knowledge that it will be one-color and integrate that into the design concept itself. The result is a more creative, ingenious attitude on the part of the designer, and dynamic self-promotion pieces at a fraction of the "normal" cost.

The twenty-seven interviews in this book feature graphic designers and illustrators from across the United States and Canada. They range from beginners to "old" pros, from one-person studios to multi-staff firms. Their common thread is that they have used their design talent and ingenuity to create successful self-promotion pieces on a low budget. The pleasant outcome is that, more often than not, these pieces stand out from the crowd on the potential client's desk, a refreshing example of strong concept, outstanding design and simplicity, among a daily barrage of color that doesn't say anything.

I hope you enjoy reading about and learning from these creative individuals as much as I did writing about them. Use the tips and information here so that your self-promotion pieces will be remembered as outstanding and different from the rest.

—Sally Prince Davis

Table of Contents

Section I

Self-Promotion: Truth, Tricks and Tips

Two types of self-promotion—indirect and direct—are vital to keeping your business alive. This section of the book discusses both: the indirect influence— how you conduct business, the quality of your product, and the reputation that you build within your community, all of which affect your total business image; and direct—the tangible promotion pieces you send to current and potential clients. Here are ideas to help you to find your niche in the marketplace, to develop two- and three-dimensional promotions, and to keep these direct promotion pieces low-cost and successful. Combine these ideas with your own creativity to create unique—and low-cost—self-promotion campaigns.

What Is Self-Promotion?

Self-promotion is *everything* you do within your business world, from how you answer the phone to how well you solve your client's design problems. It embraces all aspects — your business image, your reputation, your product, your portfolio and your promotion pieces. Self-promotion can be both indirect and direct; each kind is important.

Indirect Self-Promotion: Establishing Your Business Image

Indirect self-promotion includes all those intangibles that, combined, create your business image. How you conduct your business is an indirect self-promotion effort worth examining — are you promoting yourself to your best advantage? The graphic designer who arrives at a meeting with an organized portfolio of materials directed specifically to his or her potential client conveys a different message than the designer who spills a haphazard collection of pieces over the client's desk to "show what I've done." Work that arrives on a client's desk on time *builds* a designer's reputation as surely as unacceptable work that is inexcusably late *tears it down*. Most clients don't care how large your studio space is, but they do care how you approach them and how you solve their design problems. The overall effect of *how you work* helps to establish your business image.

> *How you conduct your business is an indirect self-promotion effort worth examining — are you promoting yourself to your best advantage?*

Even the "routine" business materials you use can promote you:

• Business correspondence that is articulately written and neatly typed on your letterhead tells this client that you are familiar with *his or her* world and with business, and you are able to move comfortably within both.

• Promptly delivered, clearly written project estimates and invoices show organization and responsibility, two qualities most clients consider mandatory in business.

• A coordinated letterhead system presents a visually unified package to the client and conveys a positive message about the seriousness of your business commitment.

• A thoughtful thank-you note, holiday greeting or special occasion announcement makes your client aware of how important he or she is to you.

Word-of-Mouth Promotion

Customer satisfaction is the key to word-of-mouth referrals, an immensely powerful type of promotion. A happy, successful client is always going to say good things about you and your work, just as a dissatisfied client will likely do the opposite. There is nothing nicer than having a new client *find you*, rather than the other way around. Time and again, word-of-mouth promotion is listed as one of the best ways to obtain clients. Referrals from one satisfied customer act as a catalyst to bring others to you.

Another avenue for word-of-mouth promotion is to build a strong, recognizable reputation within your community and among your peers. Though it may or may not lead *directly* to clients, you allow yourself and your work to be seen within the community so that the public understands, relates and hopefully responds.

This avenue of self-promotion includes:

• Entering local, regional or national competitions sponsored by art director clubs and magazines, such as *Print* and *How*.

• Doing pro bono work for nonprofit organizations.

• Speaking to organizations, in schools, or at business functions, particularly those with the best networking opportunities.

- Teaching a class.
- Making a donation to a charitable cause.

Your goal is to have contact with the community so that you become known and respected, and are the first person potential clients think of when they have design work.

Joining professional trade or business organizations, sending out press releases to local newspapers and magazines, and attending social events are other ways to cheaply and painlessly get the word around about who you are and what you do. Some of these activities could also lead to an award or other form of recognition that will boost your business image.

However, a word of caution. Don't depend solely on word-of-mouth referrals to obtain clients. Even the most satisfied clients drift away at times for reasons sometimes not even known to them. Relying totally on word of mouth can leave your studio high and dry if the referrals slow down, and you suddenly realize that no one else knows of your existence. A sudden rush to do direct self-promotion will be ineffective because it takes time for self-promotion to build and reap name recognition. The best of all worlds is to keep your name visible and your products and services out in the marketplace, while also basking in the work from a healthy word-of-mouth clientele. Self-promotion continuity is the key; don't wait until you're without business to begin to create it.

Direct Self-Promotion: Connecting With Potential Clients

The goals of *direct self-promotion* are to get new clients, refresh the memories of former clients, and keep your business name in the marketplace. Direct self-promotion revolves around the physical self-promotion pieces that you mail, deliver or present to clients, and can be the fastest way to connect to potential clients. These self-promotion pieces work hard for you in your absence; therefore, you must give them a great deal of thought and pay attention to the smallest details.

Before you begin to design these direct self-promotion pieces, you must know what business image you want to convey and the types of projects you *want* to attract. Perhaps you know, for example, that you want an image of being the studio that's easygoing and filled with innovative, challenging ideas. You also want to do "fun" projects, ones that are less conservative in their use of humor, color or typeface. In this circumstance, your promotion pieces must be bouncy and cheerful—an indicator of the mood of the studio—while displaying how well you incorporate color, humor or type to create an eye-catching and unusual piece. You want clients to know that you are confident of your talent and ability to solve their design problems.

> **Customer satisfaction is the key to word-of-mouth referrals, an immensely powerful type of promotion.**

Perhaps your business image is not that clear cut in your mind, however. You consider yourself a good designer, but haven't found your niche in the marketplace yet. How do you start to plan a promotion piece? On a piece of paper:

1. List your creative strengths and the specific services you want to provide.

2. List what you enjoy and want to make money doing, for example, corporate identity development or package design.

> **Self-promotion continuity is the key; don't wait until you're without business to begin to create it.**

3. Determine the general market areas where your talents and interests fit best, for example, publishing, advertising or public relations.

4. List the kinds of businesses within those areas

© 1991 Michael Schwab Design

that are most open to the services you offer and that are the types of firms you want to approach.

Now you know *what* you are offering clients and *who* those clients are. Begin your initial promotion design by rendering two or three promotion pieces, each focusing on one of your strengths and/or services and each directed to one type of business. Concentrate on communicating to this specific clientele how you can help them, why your strength or service is ideal for them, and urge them to take some action (preferably to call you). As you work through and refine these practice pieces, you will become clearer about who you are as a designer, what your business offers, and which types of businesses you are most comfortable approaching. As you solve some of your own promotion design problems, you'll discover even more answers to what you want your business image to be and the types of projects you want to attract.

Also try role-playing. Visualize yourself as one of your target clients and determine what special message and format would appeal to you. Perhaps as a designer, you're a one-person studio and enjoy working with very small businesses. Picture yourself as one of these small-business clients and determine some of the problems you might be encountering. Use these as a common thread to the service you can supply as a problem solver. The result might be a promotion card that begins with "I understand the problems of the one-person business. I'm one too." You've set up an immediate rapport with this new client; follow through by stating the service you can provide, always addressing the concerns of the small-business person.

Always target your pieces to the cli-

ents *most likely* to need your service. For example, if you want "fun" projects, contact game and toy manufacturers, greeting card companies, premium companies, advertising agencies, and so on. However, keep in mind that if your studio becomes viewed by others as having a narrow creative perspective, it's not going to be easy to change it down the road. Consider carefully the image you're projecting and the type of clientele you're approaching. Can images change? Of course, but it isn't always easy. If you want to enter a market area that demands an image very different from the one you've established, make sure your promotional message as well as your portfolio presentation shows this new direction. If your reputation is widely known, it might be a tough sell until you obtain those first few clients who are satisfied with your product.

Types of Promotion Pieces

A *two-dimensional* printed promotion piece is the one most commonly used by artists. These printed pieces can be:

- a letterhead system including business cards
- a self-mailer postcard
- a panel card mailed in an envelope
- a folded card mailed in an envelope
- a one-page flyer
- a multi-page brochure
- a folded or spiral-bound booklet
- a flip book
- a résumé
- a reply card
- a newspaper
- a newsletter
- bookmarks
- a poster

A letterhead, envelope and business card should be the first pieces you produce. A well-designed letterhead can also function as an estimate or billing form, thus keeping costs down. For example, Tom Scott, president of the Art of Business in West Conshohoken, Pennsylvania, creates all of his business forms on his stationery's second sheets by using his computer and laser printer. Designer Karen Lehman of Salem, Massachusetts, produces colorful invoices on her letterhead with her photocopier and color toner cartridges.

A logo or graphic element used consistently throughout your two-dimensional pieces ties together diverse items, unifies a package, and creates the impression of a prepared, well-organized individual. The development of the "right" look for your letterhead is one of the hardest jobs you give yourself, but it's absolutely worth the effort. Often this is the first design of yours that a potential client sees. If it conveys the business image you seek, you're not only telling that person about yourself and your business, but also giving him insight into how you solve design problems.

Other pieces, to be successful, should be created with an equally definite purpose in mind. If the goal of a postcard is to woo back former clients, let its message reflect that. A flyer to ad agencies should present design and copy geared to that field. Understand *why* you send out a specific piece to help you make it its most effective.

Three dimensional pieces are being used by more and more artists to capture the attention of potential clients. Although appearing more elaborate than two-dimensional pieces, they can still be inexpensively produced. Three-dimensional pieces can include gifts at holiday time, such as T-shirts or spice holders; or be clever, straightforward reminders of the existence of your studio, such as three-dimensional objects that the client assembles, or calendars. Pictogram Studio in Washington, DC, developed a three-part, three-dimensional campaign involving wordplay and miniature objects in boxes. Designer Shari Smith

of Worthington, Ohio, designed calendars that are mailed flat but then assembled by the client to sit on the desk. All of these items become "keepers," pieces that remain with the client for a long time.

Often not part of a mass mailing because of financial considerations, these items are mailed or hand delivered to the most cherished clients or those you're most eager to work with. To keep costs down on your three-dimensional promotion, contact craft supply or jewelry supply stores for small, inexpensive boxes. Design your piece so that "printed" pieces can actually be photocopied or handpainted. Instead of paying for die-cutting, hand cut pieces yourself or enlist the help of friends and family. Use excess supplies from your studio, trade-offs with vendors, and creative/production ingenuity to create special promotions for as little as a dollar apiece.

Opportunities for Special Occasion Promotion

Any special occasion is an ideal opportunity to promote yourself and your studio. Specialized mailings can be sent out for the holidays (don't forget, there are more holidays than Christmas and New Year's—ever consider a Fourth of July greeting to bolster name recognition during the summer doldrums?), as invitations to a party, announcements of a new address, awards, or staff additions—indeed, any circumstance can provide a reason to contact clients. Canadian designer Catharine Bradbury used a summer trip abroad to develop two mailers. One she sent to clients announcing the upcoming trip and urging them to contact her with design projects so they could be

© 1989 Gina Federico Graphic Design

Gina Federico | Graphic Design
134 Main Street, New Canaan, CT 06840
phone + fax 203 966-9457
PLEASE NOTE NEW ADDRESSES

Gina Federico
The Ogden House
40 Ogden Road
New Canaan CT
06840 USA
203 966-7603

Margaret Mitchell
USA 1

When designer Gina Federico of New Canaan, Connecticut, moved both her home and studio to new locations, she needed change-of-address cards—fast—because of an upcoming American Institute of Graphic Arts conference in Texas. Her solution was to buy a box of Rolodex cards and a rubber stamp designed to look like a postal cancellation stamp. Both of her new addresses and phone numbers are included within the cancellation stamp. A one-cent postage stamp completes the postal theme. The Rolodex card allowed the new addresses to be easily filed and kept by art directors.

completed before she left. The second was mailed on her return to announce that she was back and filled with new ideas.

Two-dimensional special occasion mailings tend to be large (more than a hundred names) because you're not targeting a specific client or project type, rather you're simply spreading good cheer while increasing name recognition. Because of the financial savings in both printing and postage, postcards, panel cards and folded cards are often created for these mailings, though this is certainly not a hard-and-fast rule. Sayles Graphic Design in Des Moines, Iowa, creates unique three-dimensional party invitations to mail out to more than two hundred people to celebrate the local Addy awards presentation.

Definitely utilize specialized mailings to keep clients apprised of your business changes. It is a common, and big, mistake to not keep *all* people informed when you change your address or phone number. You always want to be reachable. Don't miss out on a client's job, the opportunity to be featured in a magazine or book, or an unexpected price break on a vendor's paper stock.

In fact, the move to a new studio or the addition of staff members can be the occasion to hold a party and to introduce the public to your new surroundings, equipment and staff. Existing and potential clients don't often have the opportunity to see the graphic design business "at work." An open house can provide the perfect circumstance to show clients how your skills and/or equipment can solve their specific identity or marketing problem. Artists often give visitors a low-cost gift such as a notepad, pencil holder, a poster or even a coupon good for a discount on the first job, as a thank you for coming. This type of piece can keep your name in front of them long after the party is over.

All promotion pieces, whether two-dimensional or three-dimensional, carry subliminal messages through their appearance and targeting. Pay attention to details. A sloppy piece ("It was just for me, so I didn't care what it looked like") informs the client that you might take the same attitude toward his work. A cutesy image ("Let's have fun together") sent to the head of a corporate investment firm barks that you didn't do your homework about the type of work this client most likely wants.

Buying Ads in Creative Sourcebooks

Ads in creative sourcebooks, such as *Madison Avenue Handbook* and *Creative Black Book*, are direct self-promotion options. This avenue isn't recommended if you're on a limited budget, because these ads are expensive. However, when you reach the time that your self-promotion budget allows exploration of new areas, consider them. These books are filled with ads created by and paid for by artists/designers and contain excellent examples of their work. The consumers of the books are art directors, which means your work is seen by numerous purchasers of design simultaneously.

To get the most out of your ad, write or call the publisher of the book you're most interested in and request rate and demographic information. Then ask three questions:

1. Who is the book distributed to?
2. Is it distributed free or is it purchased?
3. Do you receive reprints of the ad free or at a charge?

The answers you receive will help you choose the book that will go to the audience best for your work, will get you the widest distribution for your money, and will give you tearsheets for your own self-promotion. Keep in mind black-and-white ads cost less than color; the larger the size of your ad the higher the fee; and regional books tend to be less expensive than those with national distribution.

Producing a 3-D Promotion

**Marty Ittner
Graphic Designer
Washington, D.C.**

Designer Marty Ittner's Coniferous Christmas card evolved from a desire to "have a two-dimensional card that would turn into a three-dimensional object." The idea to create a cone-shaped Christmas tree that could be mailed flat and assembled by the recipient was generated by her niece's birthday party hats. Ittner's first call was to the U.S. National Arboretum where tree samples were collected and tagged for her, so she could place numerous types of conifers on her card complete with correct labeling. Then "I had to find some paper that was a dark green and text weight, which was difficult, because dark papers are usually cover weight." The paper was located at an art supply store. The black type is photocopied onto the tree and the white tree

samples are silkscreened, as is the inside message. Folding instructions and self-adhesive dots are included inside.

A template for the "arc" of the card helped speed the cutting process for Ittner, who also scored and folded the card by hand. Executed completely in-house except for the photocopying, the card stayed within the two-hundred-dollar limit Ittner had set as her card budget. The one thing she did notice, however, was that as a staff designer, when you're holding down a full-time job, you need "to start the production process early. I started the card in August and finished it in December. In giving myself enough time, I was able to do it in a leisurely fashion, which enhanced the quality without making me feel I was enslaved to it. If you can put it down for a couple of days and pick it up again, you can stay friends with it."

An inexpensive two-dimensional Christmas card becomes a unique three-dimensional decoration.

© Marty Ittner

Low-Cost Self-Promotion

The term "low-cost" is relative—it depends on how many pieces you're creating, the purpose of the piece, and your budget for the entire project. Within this book, the actual costs to produce low-cost pieces range from a few pennies to several dollars apiece. Perhaps, therefore, low-cost defines any situation where through innate creativity and ingenuity you contrive to pay less in actual money than you would have if you had not instituted some cost-cutting measures.

Design and Production Tricks

You can cut costs in numerous ways. Some "tricks" to keep in mind when designing your promotion pieces are:
• One-color ink on color paper creates the illusion of two-color printing.
• Print on only one side, fold the unprinted half to the inside and glue the piece to create the illusion of two-sided printing.
• Hand cut pieces rather than paying for die-cutting.
• Have staff or family members hand-assemble pieces in-house to save bindery costs.
• Determine if you really must have a piece offset printed—perhaps photocopying or silkscreening is more appropriate and cheaper.
• Consider designing a piece that's entirely written text, using humor and wordplay to "paint the picture" as San Diego, California, designer Collette Murphy did on her series of three mailers. If you're able to produce type in-house, the piece is even more cost-effective.
• Combine printing methods—a basic piece offset printed or photocopied in black ink can have color added through sponge painting, rubber or gummed stamps at little or no cost.

Let your ingenuity rise to the surface when money is limited.

Working closely with your printer is one of the best cost-efficient practices you can develop. Ask questions, whether the job is for you or for your client. You won't know how the printer is planning to lay out a particular job until you ask. Sometimes extra pieces will fit onto a page because the original job (yours or a client's) doesn't fill the whole sheet of paper. If the job is for a client, talk to him to see if he wants to use that extra space. If not, ask if you can "tag on" to the print run. You pay your share of the film costs, but the printing and paper are essentially free. Of course you're limited to the paper and ink colors the client is using, but for nearly free promotional pieces, these "obstacles" simply become design considerations.

Ask your printer what paper he has "on the floor." Sometimes jobs are cancelled or reduced in quantity and the printer is left with overstock, which he's willing to discount to get rid of it. If the type and quantity of the overstock fit a client's project needs, suggest the paper to him and point out the savings. Or look at your own self-promotion schedule to see if you can use it. If you save your client money, he'll think you're wonderful. If you're saving yourself money, you *are* wonderful.

High-tech Conveniences

Technology makes many low-cost self-promotion pieces producible entirely in-house. Design, type and finished pieces are computer-generated and laser printed without an artist ever leaving the studio. Even if your printer isn't of sufficient quality to produce final copy, a computer allows you to work and rework the concept of your piece until you have exactly what you want.

Be aware, however, of the limitations of laser printing. Design your piece so the equipment and reproduction method you use are in line with the final quality you're seeking.

Most desktop laser printers print out at 300 dots per inch (dpi). For single pieces such as an invoice or a proposal, this low-resolution laser printing is absolutely satisfactory. However, if you're producing final copy for a piece to be reproduced in quantity, this type of laser printing produces the best results using small (12 point and smaller) type sizes and a less expensive method of reproduction such as laser copying or photocopying. Larger type sizes and other printing methods can be used, of course, but watch for letters that appear broken and have fuzzy edges due to the low dpi of the original. Laser printers using 800 and 1,200 dpi are on the market and produce sharper images, which increases their versatility within the studio setting. For the maximum laser-printed quality on your pieces, a service bureau can output your final copy at a high-resolution 2,400 dpi. There is a cost, of course, but your typesize and printing options are nearly limitless. For the crispest type, turn to the photo-typesetter.

Computer design and laser printing can also increase the versatility of your pieces. Information within one basic piece can be changed as needed to accommodate a move, a different targeted market, or changes in staff. For example, designer M. Brooks Greene, Port Orange, Florida, had her letterhead and business cards offset printed without an address or phone number because of an upcoming move. Both old and new addresses and phone numbers were added as needed by running the letterhead and cards through a laser printer.

Photocopiers and laser copiers have revolutionized quick printing today. Quick-print shops can reproduce your pieces for a fraction of the cost of offset printers and provide satisfactory multiple illustrations and text for both two-dimensional and three-dimensional promotion pieces. These copies can be used in conjunction with other elements, which is what designer Tom Graham of Kemptville, Ontario, did when he reproduced the type and line drawing for the inside of a pop-up

promotion piece on a photocopier. Or quick printing can produce the entire promotion, such as when Brooklyn, New York, illustrator Susan Greenstein created numerous mailers by having her black-and-white pieces photocopied and her color illustrations laser copied.

One of the greatest advantages to copying your self-promotion piece is that you can produce only as many copies as you need — no more thousands of useless pieces collecting dust under the bed. And you can reproduce them whenever you desire — if you run short of a piece that's eliciting a tremendous response, you simply copy more. The price per page for the copying service is minimal, and designing your layout so that you're copying two-up, four-up or even more, reduces the price per piece dramatically.

Don't overlook the advantages of owning a home copier. Not only can you produce quick black-and-white copies, but you can color print with color toner cartridges. Though some limitations exist because of the smaller size of most home copiers, investigate if this piece of equipment can meet your needs and eliminate those quick-print service fees.

Trade-offs and Collaboration

Trade-offs are common to obtain services without paying cash. It's the old barter system where you trade your design services for the service or product the other person is offering, most frequently printing, paper or typesetting. When seeking this

© 1990 Deborah K. Austin

FINDING A HARDWORKING, CREATIVE, DESIGNER IS EASIER THAN YOU MAY THINK...

ALL IT TAKES IS PUSHING THE RIGHT BUTTONS.

I have recently graduated from San Diego State University with a degree in Graphic Design. I would love the opportunity to show you my portfolio.

DEBORAH AUSTIN

Graphic designer Deborah Austin of La Mesa, California, developed this low-cost mailer when seeking employment. Printed in black, on white lightweight cardstock, the piece was reproduced at a quick printer for approximately thirty cents a piece. The trifold promotion was heavy enough to be mailed out as a self-mailer, thereby saving the expense of an envelope. Austin slipped a résumé inside. A mailing of sixty-five pieces resulted in two calls within two days. Also, the mailer can be used again — alone or with other pieces — until she changes her phone number.

arrangement, turn to the vendors you use often. These are the people with whom you've built up a trust level and reputation. Usually a trade-off involves a credit line as part of the bargain, but not always; sometimes the vendor is willing to trade merely as a thank you for business or service you've given him in the past.

If you're considering a trade-off, do your best to limit yourself to supplying a service that is relatively equal in value to what is being given to you. Resentment builds if either party feels "taken," and such a trade-off can end a good working relationship. Be clear about what you're trading so that no one ends up with an unpleasant surprise. If your trade-off with a printer includes paper, be sure it's the type of paper you want or that what he's offering is something you're willing to accept. Often, a trade-off with a printer is for the printing only or a willingness to forget his markup on the paper, thus selling it to you at his cost.

Designers, writers, illustrators or photographers often collaborate on a piece to cut costs. Whether it's a holiday greeting that you and another professional send out together or an entire brochure that features several professionals, a more elaborate piece can be produced because each person picks up a portion of the total cost or contributes material to create the piece. It's wisest to consider a collaborative piece with related, but different, professions so as not to be in direct competition with each other. Another benefit to this approach is that you can combine mailing lists, weed out the duplicates, and, depending on the number of collaborators, double, triple or even quadruple

> **Setting realistic self-promotion goals enables you to budget your time, money and effort so that your self-promotion is consistent, not a flurry of activity squeezed in between other projects.**

your exposure because all of you are distributing the piece.

Planning Your Promotion Strategy

Consider a promotion strategy as a road map that gets you to your destination by the most direct route, saving you time and money. This map lets you plan your stops, stay on course, and arrive feeling satisfied that you've reached your goal and that it's been a good trip.

With your promotion strategy, the destination is the achievement of your self-promotion goals for the year. Increased name recognition, market positioning, peer recognition, the winning of at least one award, a new client base, a new perception of your business, increased revenues—all of these are legitimate goals for your self-promotion to fulfill. Follow these three steps to reach your goals:

1. Choose your most important goals.

2. Set your budget.

3. Schedule your mailings.

4. Evaluate the results.

Choose Your Most Important Goals

Be realistic. Although all of the goals mentioned above are desirable, select only those that are the most important to you. Setting realistic self-promotion goals enables you to budget your time, money and effort so that your self-promotion is consistent, not a flurry of activity squeezed in between other projects. Evaluate the time and money you have to invest to reach these chosen goals. The more dramatic the goal, the greater your investment needs to be. For example, wanting only to increase your revenues doesn't necessarily mean turning to a whole new type of client or changing your business image. It can mean merely enlarging your mailing list and increasing the number of pieces you send out per mailing to reach more potential clients. But if you *are* trying to attract a totally new type of client, your investment needs to be greater because new promotion pieces will have to be designed, client research undertaken, and new samples placed in the portfolio. By selecting the one or two goals most important to you now, you can focus on those, achieve that success, and let others come along as side benefits.

Now that you know where you're heading, you can begin to plan how to get there in the most economical and timely ways.

Establish a Promotion Budget

A general rule of thumb is to set aside 10 percent of your business income to cover your self-promotion costs. Though sometimes difficult to do, having a specific amount of money to work with lets you plan your campaign so it doesn't fizzle out in the middle and lets you know how much you can spend per piece. This allows you to solve your marketing problems creatively within budget parameters.

Self-promotion is somewhat of a financial paradox — the less work you have, the more you should be promoting yourself. In fact, recessionary times are when you should cut back on everything but your advertising. If anything you should advertise more. By socking away your self-promotion dollars a little every month, you can take advantage of the lean times by getting your name out there when your colleagues are pulling in to save dollars.

Budgeting time is as important as budgeting money. Many designers admit that they do self-promotion only when things get slow in the office because that is when they have the time. A regular self-promotion project schedule will mean fewer slow times. No, the payment isn't immediate as with your clients, but the payoff is in more consistent jobs down the road. Consistency within a self-promotion plan is one of the most valuable habits you can acquire. Nothing is more ineffective than a one-shot promotion.

Schedule Your Mailings

You should plan a year's worth of promotion. The benefits to a year-long promotion strategy are: 1) You can plan an overall theme always aimed toward your long-range goal; 2) You can build one piece on another to give continuity to your efforts; 3) Clients see your staying power in the industry; 4) You feel productive and in control of your career.

> **A general rule of thumb is to set aside 10 percent of your business income to cover your self-promotion costs.**

To set up your year-long schedule, sit down with your long-range goals and a calendar. Analyze the market field you're approaching. Every business has a rhythm of slow and busy periods — you want your mailings to land on the art director's desk just as he's starting to plan projects for his busy time. Then:

1. *Select and produce your pieces.* Viewing the year as a whole, decide the frequency with which you will have to mail to achieve your goals. This might be once a month or every three months. Decide whether special occasion mailings will be tied thematically to your planned, goal-oriented campaign. Keeping your financial parameters in mind, determine the specific types of pieces you'll create. Perhaps a series of low-cost, accordion-fold cards mailed every two months culminating in a gift at Christmas. Or perhaps a calendar but one that is designed to be mailed every three months (three months on

> **Self-promotion is somewhat of a financial paradox — the less work you have, the more you should be promoting yourself.**

Making Pro Bono Work Pay

David Levy
David Levy Design, Inc.
Atlanta, Georgia

David Levy approaches pro bono work with the same common sense he brings to his business. "If you're working with a group that's going to produce fifty little brochures for only its membership, that's not a very effective self-promotion vehicle for yourself. But if you produce a poster for a playhouse in town that's going to be in windows all over the city, that's much better use of self-promotion." For a newcomer to the field, pro bono work can be a foot in the door as well as provide a certain credibility to talent. "Many times when you do pro bono work for groups, you're dealing with people in corporate positions that have leads or can give you paying work in the future. It allows your work to be seen by them."

The business side of this type of work is as important as any other contract with a client, perhaps more so. When your "pay" is the credit line, the final piece must truly represent your work, or the value of the credit line diminishes proportionately. Levy talks with the client up front and lets them know that because it is pro bono that "they have to give a little more trust than with a paying job. I have some very strict guidelines when I do pro bono work. I have a contract that clients sign when I do paying work, and I have a different letter of agreement for pro bono work — they cannot make changes to the work except factual or grammatical changes without consulting me. I make sure I get credit for it, but if it's not produced excellently, it's not worth it. I really don't want my name on it if it's not going to look good."

Membership in the Art Director's Club of Atlanta, now the Creative Club of Atlanta, provided an opportunity for pro bono work, which Levy saw as "an opportunity to do some self-promotion material and to get some good PR as well as peer recognition, which is very important in this industry. I've been active in the club, serving on the executive committee and other committees since I've been in Atlanta. I went to them and asked to do the newsletter for the next year."

An example of the commitment Levy had to the project was the final edition of the newsletter for the year. It was printed in three colors throughout, credit lines were exchanged for copywriting, design, production, type output, illustration, photography and paper. The piece was designed as a self-mailer to avoid the cost of envelopes, and the layout and camera-ready artwork were prepared on a Macintosh computer. Levy also produced the twenty-four-page club membership directory pro bono as well and kept it cost-effective with computer preparation, credit lines for services, and one-color printing. Each alphabetic category within the directory is introduced with an illustration, design or photograph.

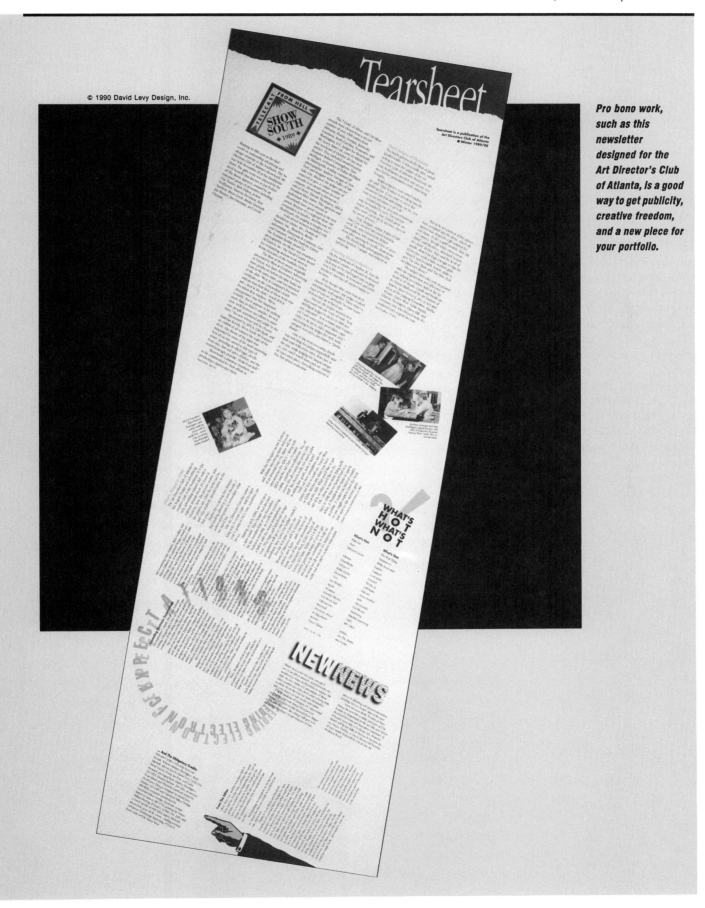

Pro bono work, such as this newsletter designed for the Art Director's Club of Atlanta, is a good way to get publicity, creative freedom, and a new piece for your portfolio.

FAX TRANSMITTAL
from Barbara Kelley
533 Main Street / Northport, NY 11768
516-754-7374 FAX: 516-757-2553

Number of Pages: Date:

To: Time:

Memo:

© Barbara Kelley

each calendar sheet) so that your name is constantly in front of the client.

Once you decide the type of campaign you're going to produce, set mailing dates. Then, regardless of whether you are planning a simple mailer or a complex calendar, set up a production schedule complete with worksheet, budget, and most important, a deadline for its completion.

2. *Maintain your mailing lists.* Keep potential and current client names and addresses up to date. To easily target your mailings, use a card file or your computer database and keep client mailings organized by type of market. For example, use one code for advertising agencies, another for public relations firms, and so on; list separately special clients you want to remember with a unique thank you, invitation or gift.

Computers also dramatically speed up the production of mailings. Labels print out at a moment's notice, eliminating much of this self-promotion drudgery. If you're buying mailing lists, ask questions and invest your money wisely. Buy only lists that are culled to reflect the specific market and/or geographic area you want to approach. Ask the price of receiving pre-printed labels — the extra fee might be worth the time you'll save.

3. *Activate your mailings.* Stick to your schedule religiously so your mailings reach the clients as you planned. When finished with a mailing, don't be discouraged if it doesn't attract a client immediately. More often than not, it is your continuous effort that finally brings a client around to you. Luck (your piece arrived the day the art director was seeking a fresh "look") and timing (your piece arrived the day the ad agency was deluged with new projects) play almost as much a part in getting that job as does the content of your mailing. Therefore, the more

you have your name out there, the more you increase your chances of making contact at "just the right time."

4. *Evaluate the results.* Depending on the frequency of your mailings, you may be ready to evaluate their results after six months; if this is too soon for the campaign you've planned, wait until your year of self-promotion is completed. The main question to answer is, did I achieve my long-range goals? Whether your answer is yes or no, ask one further question — why or why not? The answer to this question tells you what you're doing right or wrong. Review when you received the projects you were seeking and when you were your busiest. Determine if these circumstances occurred after one of your self-promotion mailings. Use all of the information from this campaign to begin to plan your next one.

Commitment and organization are the keys to successful self-promotion; without them, your self-promotion efforts will be nebulous and marginally effective. Most important, treat yourself and your promotion project as you would a client with a paying job.

The Merits of Pro Bono Work

The amount of time and effort necessary to create name recognition depends, of course, on the size of your community. Given equal amounts of effort, you will see faster results in Akron, Ohio, than you will in Manhattan. But regardless of whether you're attacking Akron or Manhattan, high visibility not only is a wonderful ego stroke when someone compliments you on a job, but it also creates a sense of expertise, a credibility if you will, to your business and your talent.

Pro bono work, work that you do for free, is one way to acquire high visibility while creating a low-cost self-promotion piece. Associations and non-profit organizations, such as theater and dance groups, hospitals, animal protection leagues, libraries and support groups, are often open to the idea of a graphic designer or an illustrator creating a special project. The organization usually picks up the expenses—paper, typesetting, printing and so on. The graphic designer receives a credit line and, sometimes, samples. The result is a highly visible example of your work seen by the public at little or no cost to you.

The key to pro bono work is to do a project that is definitely going to be seen by a lot of people. Look for projects with broad interest such as a poster on saving a local landmark. Work on something you really believe in. It makes the donation of your time and effort more meaningful. If possible, join the organization. Often the board members of these associations are the movers and shakers of the community, people who own businesses or are financially influential. Working with them on an issue of personal interest is bound to make an impact and can possibly lead to a client relationship. If nothing else, should you decide to approach them as potential clients someday, the piece you designed is a wonderful way to break the ice.

A brochure to twenty-five members of an organization is not going to get you the publicity you need. However, designing or illustrating a club directory or newsletter is beneficial when it's for your own graphic art association. This type of work distinguishes you from other members and creates

peer recognition and acceptance. Networking for client leads within your peer group becomes easier because you can point to the pro bono project as an example of your work.

When performing a pro bono job, get as much creative freedom as you can since you want this piece to be an outstanding example of *your* work. Encourage your client to oversee the informational content, leaving the creative areas to you. You can then be sure that the design remains true to your vision and faithfully reflects your talent.

Speaking engagements and volunteer teaching may present opportunities to design promotional materials for the event. When invited to share your expertise, ask if the sponsor is willing to bear the expense of printing a poster or brochure to advertise the occasion if you are willing to design it for free. You can also suggest working with a printer who might contribute his materials or eliminate his markup in exchange for a credit line. Sometimes organizations will make back their expenses by selling a promotional poster to attendees. This type of poster or brochure provides you with increased visibility and an example of your work.

Speaking of Opportunity

Rex Peteet
Sibley Peteet Design
Dallas, Texas

Speaking engagements offered the perfect opportunity for Sibley Peteet Design to embark on a long-held self-promotion plan at no direct cost to the firm. Partners Rex Peteet and Don Sibley had been wanting to create a series of posters of salt and pepper shakers to play off the S and P in the firm's initials. The right circumstances to initiate the endeavor arose when they were asked to be guest speakers for the Tulsa, Oklahoma, art directors' club. Rex Peteet explains that "they approached us and said, 'We always give speakers the opportunity to design the announcement to the membership.' At the time that was not that typical of a request, but it seemed like the time to begin our series." The result was the first poster, a colorful and illustrative set of shakers, printed as an 18 × 20⅜-inch poster. "Apparently they had worked out a deal with their suppliers that it would be pro bono or at cost," Peteet states, "but it was absolutely free to us. And they were kind enough to overrun it so that we could have a quantity to use for our purposes to promote ourselves."

The second poster was created in conjunction with a speaking engagement for the Omaha Graphic Artists Guild and was "a similar situation where they asked us to design our own announcement for their membership. At the time we were just starting to break into the computer age. We had just bought our first Macintosh, and we worked with JW Burkey who was much more fluent with the computer" to obtain the final product. The piece was reproduced as a 20½ × 17-inch poster, and another cost-free addition to the series to promote Sibley Peteet Design.

Peteet notes that "most designer/art director clubs have a series of speakers that come in throughout the year. We were just one in a series of speakers but we made the most out of each opportunity. Don and I have always tried to speak together; as partners we try to keep things equitable."

A strong proponent of entering works in shows, Peteet notes that "the best self-promotion we have ever done is in shows. Just having your work published creates a network out there, and you have no idea how strong it can be. Over the years we've become a bit more selective in what we think is really going to have the most impact. It's narrowed down to *Communication Arts* and *Graphis* magazines, Pratt Institute, and the Los Angeles and New York art director shows, and of course the AIGA shows that come along. We also support our local advertising shows, which aren't published, but are seen by our community in Texas."

Established in 1982, Sibley Peteet Design is generally most widely recognized for its retail real estate and packaging design, but Peteet wants people to know that they have a corporate side also. "Those two things are what we do a lot of—retail real estate literally from coast to coast and packaging for Milton Bradley games and Mary Kay cosmetics. Those things are so visible—for example, when you do something for Milton Bradley, millions of people are exposed to it. If you do a really nice corporate capabilities piece for an architect or real estate investment company, it is directed to a small audience and limited in exposure." To promote itself to corporate clients, "we are in the process of creating a very corporate view of Sibley Peteet as well as a very retail perception."

A speaking engagement may offer the opportunity to design a promotion piece for the lecture and, ultimately, for yourself, such as this poster designed by Sibley Peteet Design for their presentation to the Tulsa art director's club.

A series concept, such as this second salt and pepper poster design by Sibley Peteet Design for the Omaha Graphic Artists Guild, can tie your speaking promotions together and give you stronger promotion pieces.

The concept behind designer David Chiow's moving announcement grew out of his love of playing with paper that moves, using paper as a design element, and getting people involved with his promotions. Two pieces of gold Chromolux cardstock comprise the announcement—one piece measures 5⅝ × 3¾ inches, the other 9⅝ × 3¾ inches. The two pieces are held together with a gold brad through a centered O. When mailed, the card reads Chiow; when moved in a semicircle, the W becomes an M and the card reads Moved and gives Chiow's new address in Maryland Heights, Missouri. Chiow had approximately fifty cards printed in black ink at a quick printer using offset thermography. The total cost for printing, mailing envelope and brads was approximately one dollar each; assembly was done by hand in house.

© Rick Eiber Design (RED), Seattle, Washington

Designer Rick Eiber, owner of Rick Eiber Design in Seattle, Washington, initiated the creation of Northwet—four collaborative brochures—to gain exposure for his firm and to showcase talent. Costs were kept low for the 9½ × 13¾-inch publications because they were produced as a joint promotional effort on a trade-off basis. Eiber provided the design, writing and finished art; other services were provided by the printer and typesetter/stat house in exchange for copies of the brochure and a page of advertising. Other artists' work was featured within the brochures, which at least quadrupled participants' exposure as all people involved distributed the brochures to their clients.

Section II

Low-Cost Self-Promotion Success Stories

This section contains case studies of graphic designers and illustrators who have created their own dynamic low-cost direct self-promotions. Reading how others achieved success let's you see firsthand how they saved money by using one-color printing, assembling pieces in-house by hand and choosing alternative printing methods—only a few of the cost-cutting methods discussed. You, too, can create two- and three-dimensional promotions, special occasion pieces, and year-long campaigns with a minimal financial investment. Let these case studies spark your own ingenious ideas to keep your business name out in the marketplace.

A Designed Move

**M. Brooks Greene
M. Brooks Greene designs
and creations
Port Orange, Florida**

Brooks Greene designed her letterhead and business cards to encompass the diversity and changes within her life.

A 1988 graduate of North Carolina State University, Greene is focusing her full-time career ambitions on graphic design, but admits to being "at a stage where I'm trying a lot of new things," which include calligraphy, knitting and screenprinting. Currently a staff designer in Daytona Beach, she anticipates a move to Savannah, Georgia, and once the move is complete, will "try and market myself as a freelance graphic designer. I have a little experience making calls, promoting myself, and organizing my efforts, but mainly I've used those skills to find a full-time job. I'm excited about freelancing because I'll be able to do more and to pick and choose." The move also provides her the opportunity "to get into the Savannah College of Art and Design and to get a master's degree. I'll be gearing toward those two things."

Greene's immediate project, however, was to design letterhead and business cards that could be used to pursue any of her varied interests and that wouldn't have to be discarded after her move because of the address change. She wanted to have the pieces printed before the move because "I have a fairly steady income [now], and I may not when I start freelancing."

Her two-stage solution is ingenious. First, to pull together her diverse interests, she selected a visual symbol for each—a triangle and compass and a computer mouse to signify her graphic design; a ball of yarn and knitting needles to represent her hand-knitted fashions; pen nibs to reflect her calligraphy talent; and a spackling knife to represent ink being placed on a screen for printing.

Both the letterhead (page 24) and cards were printed without an address or a phone number in two custom-mix colors, teal blue and orange. Greene adds address and phone number herself. On the letterhead, all of the symbols appear throughout the sheet as pale background "decorations." On each of the business cards, however, only one symbol appears, allowing Greene to target the cards appropriately. "With the business cards, I can send cards to selected potential clients. If I really want to market my calligraphy, I can use the calligraphy business card, or if I really want to put out a line of knitted clothing, I can use the business card with the knitting symbol on it." Without the address on it, that particular card can serve as a hangtag for her fashions. Some of the cards are without icons, which allows them universal usage.

"The bill for the whole printing job was $185 including tax. To me that was a lot of money, but I can use these many different times. I only ordered two hundred of each, but the business cards are ten-up, so I actually got two thousand cards. I calculated the cost at fifty-two cents per piece, but with the business cards, it's much cheaper. I even received somewhat of a discount at the printer—he quoted me a higher price I knew I couldn't afford, and he came down. He gave me

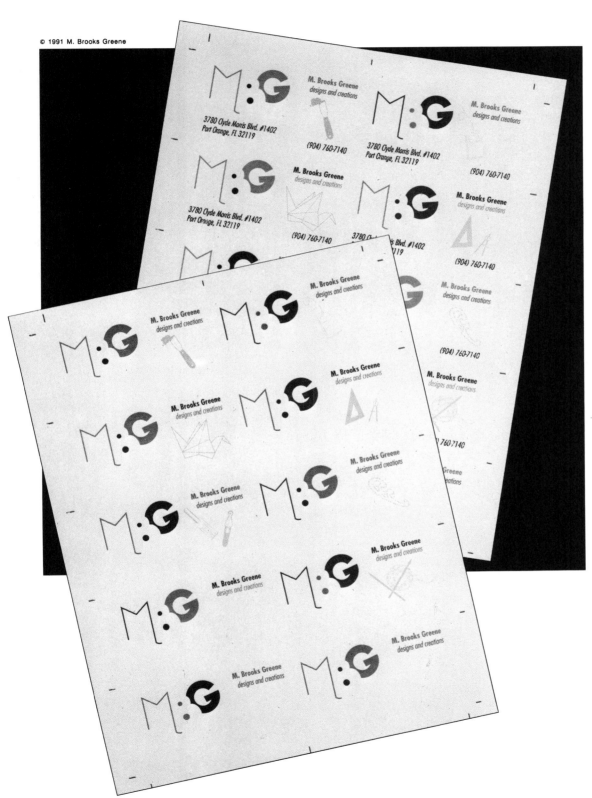

Business Card Sheets
Size:
8½ × 11 inches
Paper:
Classic Laid Cream card stock
Type:
MBG—Custom; Name—Futura Condensed Bold; designs and creations—Futura Condensed Light Oblique
Color:
Custom-mix PMS 3145 Teal and PMS 145 Orange
Printing:
Offset; address computer printed (laser and dot matrix)
Quantity:
200 sheets printed ten-up (2,000 cards)
Unit cost:
Offset printing—approximately 46 cents per sheet; Laser printing—25 cents per sheet

Letterhead

Size:
8 ½ × 11 inches
Paper:
Classic Laid Cream
Type:
MBG — Custom; Name —
Futura Condensed Bold;
designs and creations —
Futura Condensed Light
Oblique
Color:
Custom-mix PMS 3145
Teal and PMS 145 Orange
Printing:
Offset
Quantity:
200
Unit cost:
Offset printing —
approximately 46 cents per
sheet

M. Brooks Greene *designs and creations*

M. Brooks Greene
designs and creations

3780 Clyde Morris Blvd. #1402
Port Orange, FL 32119

(904) 760-7140

the negatives and the plates, so if I ever want to use them again with different colors, I can just hand them over to the print shop in Savannah. That's going to save me money down the road too."

The second stage of the problem was how to include the address information; her Macintosh computer solved that. Because the pieces were printed without an address and phone number, Greene simply adds the appropriate information as needed. She takes the letterhead and runs it through her printer, which prints out the address, phone number, and "whatever message I have on the letterhead. But the business card is printed on a heavier cardstock, so it doesn't go through the dot matrix printer very well. I take those to a computer dealer in town to be printed out on a laser printer. They charge twenty-five cents per copy, which is pretty expensive in my book. But that's still ten-up," which greatly reduces the cost per card. The advantage to the computer printing of the address is that Greene can use the pieces while still in Florida, change the pieces to reflect her new address in Georgia, and "if I ever move again or get lucky enough to open an office, I can change it to that."

Greene is already looking ahead to the day when she'll be freelancing and has her future self-promotion plans underway. "I took some off-the-wall photos a couple of months ago, and they might be fun to use as a self-promotion once I get to Savannah. I can send them out and say, here I am, I'm in town, and ready to do your work. I can do those four-up with a different photo on each one and on the back just put brief information about myself and my logo and the mailing information."

Watching expenses and sticking to a budget for self-promotion coincides with Greene's personal design philosophy: "If you can do high-quality design on a low budget, you're set. I've always felt that printing black on white is the ultimate challenge, because you have this certain-size page, and one color of ink, and you have to discover what you can possibly do with it that will make it more eye-catching than something a lot slicker. Slicker doesn't always mean better."

Keen As Mustard

Catharine Bradbury
Bradbury Design
Regina, Saskatchewan

Working in a town the size of Regina, Saskatchewan — about 200,000 — means that designer Catharine Bradbury doesn't specialize; in fact, "I have to be able to provide as many different styles as possible. I do a lot of work for nonprofit organizations and do corporate work as well. It really depends on who calls me." But that's no problem for Bradbury: "I don't mind because it gives me a good variety, and I enjoy that. I would probably get bored if I was doing only one type of work."

A one-person business, Bradbury Design was formed in 1989 after Bradbury had worked in an advertising agency for two years and spent several years freelancing on the west coast of Canada. When asked how a town the size of Regina could support more than a handful of designers, Bradbury notes that "Regina is a government town, so there is more work here than even I realized. It comes down to how you promote yourself." To start from scratch isn't easy, and the first thing Bradbury did was to develop a mailing list of names given to her by friends and business acquaintances, acquired from the phone book, and by looking through the newspaper for names of advertisers whose ads appeared to have been designed. "I sent materials out and started to see people. I probably know about one-third of my mailing list, so there's two-thirds out there I've never met," which means yet-to-be-tapped potential business.

Scheduled twice yearly, her promotion mailings are created with the same flair, imagination and attention to detail that Bradbury brings to her client's projects. "You want people to notice you and what you're doing. It's really important to be recognized right away. If someone came to me, quite frankly, they would have to give me a reason

to hire them. That's something I have always known, that you have to give someone a reason to pay attention to you."

Bradbury's beguiling "Over 25 Years in the Business" mailer was created in July 1990 with specific goals in mind: "I wanted to reinforce the visibility of my company and reach a larger market to increase operating revenue. I had three objectives: To reach all existing clients with a new promotion piece; to reach fifty potential clients; to increase business revenues fifteen percent by December 1990."

Bradbury developed the concept, designed the card, directed the photo shoot, and supervised all aspects of the card's production. Printed in black on white 80-pound cover stock, the front shows a young girl with a haircut and glasses similar to Bradbury's. Simple and clean, the card's front, in addition to the photo, contains only the names Catharine Bradbury and Bradbury Design. The back of the card bears a photo of Bradbury as she is today with a brief listing of the products the studio creates, the motto "images that soar, customers who sing," and the studio's address, phone number and logo.

Rich in appearance, the three hundred cards were actually produced for a total of $350. Expenses were kept low by using a friend's daughter as the model for the cover photo, arranging a paper donation from a local paper company, and crediting the photographer and the printer on the final piece in exchange for a reduction in their fees.

"Over 25 Years" Mailer
Size:
9 × 4⅛ Inches
Paper:
Cameo Dull 80-pound Cover
Type:
Futura Bold, Coronet Bold
Color:
Black
Printing:
Offset
Quantity:
300
Unit cost:
$1.16
Distribution:
Mailed in #10 envelopes
Mailing:
First class

"As Happy As Larry" and
"Keen As Mustard"
Mailers
Size:
5⅞ × 5⅞ inches
Paper:
Cameo Dull 80-pound
Cover
Type:
Futura Bold, Bodoni
Color:
Black
Printing:
Offset
Quantity:
600 (300 of each)
Unit cost:
$1.25
Distribution:
Mailed
Mailing:
First class

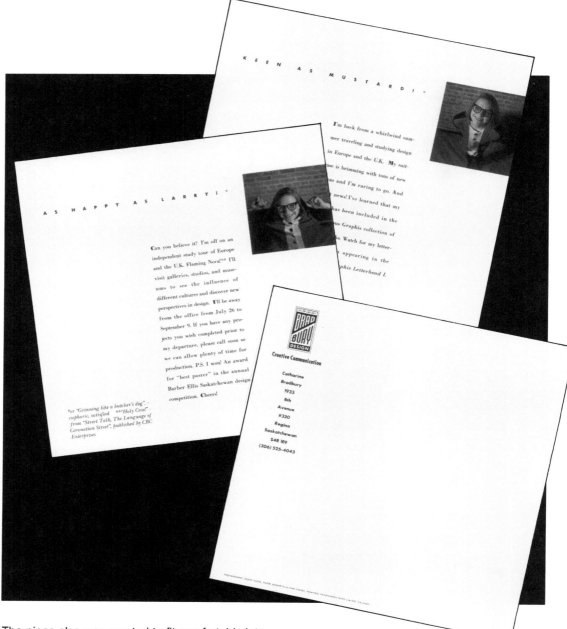

The piece also was created to fit comfortably into a standard #10 envelope so it could be mailed for first-class postage.

Bradbury not only achieved all of her stated goals, she bettered them. "My business revenue increased twenty-five percent by year's end. The card directly resulted in contracts with at least five new clients." It also won a communications award from the International Association of Business Communicators.

Acceptance into the School of Visual Arts' Arts Abroad program supplied Bradbury with another promotion opportunity. Because she planned to

be studying design in London for three weeks and to follow that with three weeks of travel in Europe, she developed two 5⅞-inch square black-and-white mailers, one announcing her departure, the other her return. Unfortunately, London's Royal College of Art cancelled the studio space for the program, but Bradbury decided to take advantage of the time for independent study and to go abroad anyway. "Luckily the cards were just at the blue line stage when I found out about the program's cancellation, so I just made some copy changes.

Easter Card
Size:
7⅜ × 3¹⁷⁄₁₈ Inches
Paper:
Lustro Dull Cream
Type:
Caslon 540
Color:
Black
Printing:
Offset
Quantity:
100
Unit cost:
50 cents (paper donation)
Distribution:
Mailed
Mailing:
First class

Not only do the mailers lift your spirits when you read them, but Bradbury crams the short text with good PR. "As Happy as Larry!" (meaning euphoric) announces Bradbury's intended study tour but also provides the opportunity for her to urge clients to call soon if they have projects they want completed before she leaves. The same mailer announces her winning an award for best poster in the Barber Ellis Saskatchewan design competition.

Her return announcement, "Keen As Mustard!" (sharp, avid, doesn't miss a trick), relates the upbeat message that she's back "with tons of new ideas and I'm raring to go." The text also tells of another honor received—inclusion of her letterhead in the "prestigious *Graphis* collection of design books." Six hundred of the cards (three hundred each) were produced for only $250: the paper was donated, printing was done at cost, and the photography and copywriting were free "by using the talents of two associates." The cards were sent out as mailers eliminating the need for envelopes.

Two other eye-catching promotions were created by Bradbury as low-cost methods of staying in touch with clients at holiday times. One, an Eas-

Holiday Greeting
Size:
6⅜ × 5¼ inches
Paper:
Environment
Type:
Futura Bold
Color:
Red, green, black
Printing:
Offset
Quantity:
300
Unit cost:
84 cents
Distribution:
Mailed
Mailing:
First class

ter card, was produced approximately five years ago in one color, because "I wanted to design a piece that would effectively use only black ink." One hundred of the offset printed cards cost only fifty dollars thanks to a paper donation and one-color printing. The second, a holiday greeting, features red and green ink with strong use of black; the three hundred self-mailer cards were produced at cost by the printer in exchange for a credit line.

Self-Promotion to Remember

Robin Seaman
Robin Seaman Design
Glendale, California

Robin Seaman possesses the self-promotion savvy of a time-proven pro even though her design firm is only two years old. She created her very first promotional brochure with a definite concept and marketing strategy, kept within her allotted budget by using cost-cutting measures, and achieved her goal of bringing in new clients.

She believes that you must "put your self-promotion project on a schedule just as you do your client's projects. Give yourself a deadline so you don't procrastinate. Design the promotion with a marketing strategy; in other words, think of it in terms of a campaign rather than a single piece. Your promotional efforts tend to be cumulative and will be much more successful if you send out several pieces every year. You want to keep your name in front of potential clients, otherwise they forget you're out there. And always, always, always follow up on everything you send out."

A 1985 graduate of UCLA with a Bachelor of Fine Arts degree in design, Seaman worked for Lockheed Corporation in its in-house design department and believes that "that experience was very valuable. Each designer within the department operated basically as a mini design firm with her own clients and projects and little interference from management. With that freedom and responsibility, I could learn and grow quickly." While working, Seaman continued her education with illustration and business courses at Art Center At Night because "my long-term goal always was to start my own business."

Seaman decided to strike out on her own in 1990, and she enjoys being a one-person operation. She feels that "at this time I prefer to keep it small. I operate out of an office in my home that is equipped with everything I could possibly need

and having a home office keeps my overhead low and my profits high."

When Seaman started to design her self-promotion brochure, she knew four things: "I wanted the promotion to be a 'keeper'; I wanted to keep the budget under $1,500; I wanted it to have a handmade quality; and I wanted it printed on recycled paper."

The concept for the brochure evolved from a play on her last name, "since it has always been something that people comment on," and the nautical theme is constant throughout, from written copy to illustrations. She used the symbolism of semaphore flags because it tied in with the sea and her last name and epitomizes visual communication.

A trifold, the brochure involves the recipient as soon as it is received, a point specifically planned by Seaman, because "research has shown that direct mail is much more effective

> *Your promotional efforts tend to be cumulative and will be much more successful if you send out several pieces every year.*

Brochure

Size:

Envelope — 7½ × 7½ inches; Brochure — closed 6⅞ × 6⅞ inches, open 6⅞ × 18⅞₆ inches; Bookmark — 6⅜ × 2 inches; Business card — 3½ × 2 inches; Mailing label — 4 × 4 inches

Paper:

Envelope — French Paper Speckletone Pueblo Dust; Brochure — French Paper Speckletone Madero Beach

Type:

Trajan, Bauer Bodoni, Avant Garde

Color:

PMS blue and gray; orange matched to envelope

Printing:

Offset

Quantity:

500

Unit cost:

$3

Distribution:

Mailed in white envelope

Mailing:

First class

when you involve the audience in the material."
With her brochure, "there are layers of paper to
deal with. Recipients have to remove it from two
envelopes (a plain envelope in which it was mailed
and a customized envelope that coordinates with
the brochure) and slide off the blue corrugated
wraparound that holds it closed. Then they open
the brochure itself which holds other elements—
two bookmarks and a business card. There's
more to it than the usual brochure and people remember it."

Seaman spells out her name on the cover with
semaphore flags, and the bookmarks inside continue the semaphore and communication symbolism. "One bookmark symbolizes the sender or client and has the image of a seaman sending a
signal using semaphore flags. This sender faces
the second bookmark that has an image of the
receiver holding a scope. The receiver symbolizes
the client's audience, which is referenced in the
accompanying copy. A lot of thought went into every element of the brochure to make sure everything ties together: the concept, the copy, the colors and the paper."

To keep the piece within budget, Seaman
worked out many of the details with her printer
before and during the design process. To keep
costs down, "all of the printed pieces were ar-
ranged on one press sheet: the mailing label,
business card, two bookmarks and brochure. The
business card and the mailing label were actually
added as an afterthought when I discovered there
was a lot of wasted space on the press sheet."
Printing is confined to one side of the sheet, another cost-cutting measure, and is then folded
over to give the appearance of two-sided printing.
This also made the piece more substantial and
helped form the pocket for insertion of the inside
bookmarks and the business card on the back.

Seaman also cut expenses significantly by
"hand cutting and assembling it. Though I doubt
I will ever take on such a time-consuming task
again, I decided that at this time I could afford the
time more than I could the money. Once the piece
was printed and scored I spent several weekends
and evenings cutting and assembling." The
printer, in exchange for a credit line on the piece,
provided one match ink and "a lot" of stripping for
free, and Seaman traded services with the copywriter—he did the work for free in exchange for
portfolio samples and her help on his next promotion.

The brochure is printed in pale shades of blue
and brown inks and possesses richness, detail
and complexity that belie its three dollar per unit
cost. Though Seaman had five hundred brochures printed, she has sent out only about seventy because "of the time required to keep up with
the follow-up calls and appointments to show my
book. Of those seventy mailed, forty people were
interested in seeing more and made appointments. Of those, four paying jobs have been generated so far, which more than paid for the cost of
the piece. It has also won an award from *HOW*
magazine as well as being included in this book,
which again are forms of self-promotion. You
should take advantage of all possibilities because
they all add up."

Seaman believes her next self-promotion piece
will tie in with the first in style and content, possibly
"two more sets of bookmarks mailed out six
months apart." Then "I would like to do something
completely different. Your own promotion pieces
give you that rare opportunity to do almost anything, budget permitting. Since you are the client,
you can get as creative as you wish."

A Brush With Color

**Karen Gourley Lehman
Lehman Graphic Design
Salem, Massachusetts**

Karen Gourley Lehman sought the best of both worlds and found it. Formerly a designer at Hewlett-Packard, she left the corporate world in 1983 to start her own business. Lehman explains the deciding factor for the move "was that I was pregnant with our first child. Even though people thought I was nuts, I decided it would be smarter for me to leave and start my freelance business before I had the baby." The formula was obviously right because she's never gone back to the corporate environment, preferring instead to integrate her work with her home life and parenting, especially now that she's the mother of three.

A designer with a broad client base, Lehman relies on being known as "a problem solver" rather than a specialist with one particular "look." She believes "you should not have a style by which you are recognizable. I think that's good if you're a photographer or illustrator, but if you do that as a designer, it tends to close doors," because not everyone is seeking the look you offer.

Lehman approached the design of her stationery and business card with the realization that these materials are the first examples of her design a client sees. "I think your stationery is an important way to put your best foot forward. If you don't do a good job for yourself, what does that say? People take things very much at face value in this field," she states. For Lehman, a perfectionist, "designing my stationery was a long process." She did "hundreds of designs and even had some of them typeset, but ultimately rejected them. After getting quotes and looking through hundreds of paper samples, I decided I wanted a super high-quality paper that was the brightest white I could find so that any color I used would be very clear, true and brilliant." She selected 100 percent rag Strathmore Ultimate White and "was assured that it was the whitest stationery stock I could purchase at the time."

To save money, she airbrushes additional color to the basic type design, which was offset printed in black: "I specified a very black ink, and I wanted the type crystal clear because some of it is very small." The graduated color block behind the black printing is added by Lehman with an airbrush and template, which is simply a right angle, "a piece of paper that has a very light adhesive on it. Every once in a while I sit down and airbrush a pile of letterheads using different colors." Her most frequently used color combination is blue/lavender, but pieces also boast green/yellow and yellow/light red, all of which draw the eye to her name and address.

Her photocopier also plays a vital role in adding color to her business materials without the cost of printing. In addition to the black toner that came with the machine, Lehman purchased canisters of red and blue toner as well. When producing her résumé and invoices, she uses her letterhead as the paper and adds new color to the pieces by photocopying them in either the red or blue toner. "Then I add my airbrushing and it looks very colorful." By using her computer to change her résumé and converting her photocopier into a printing press, Lehman easily targets her résumé to the interests of the clients she's approaching.

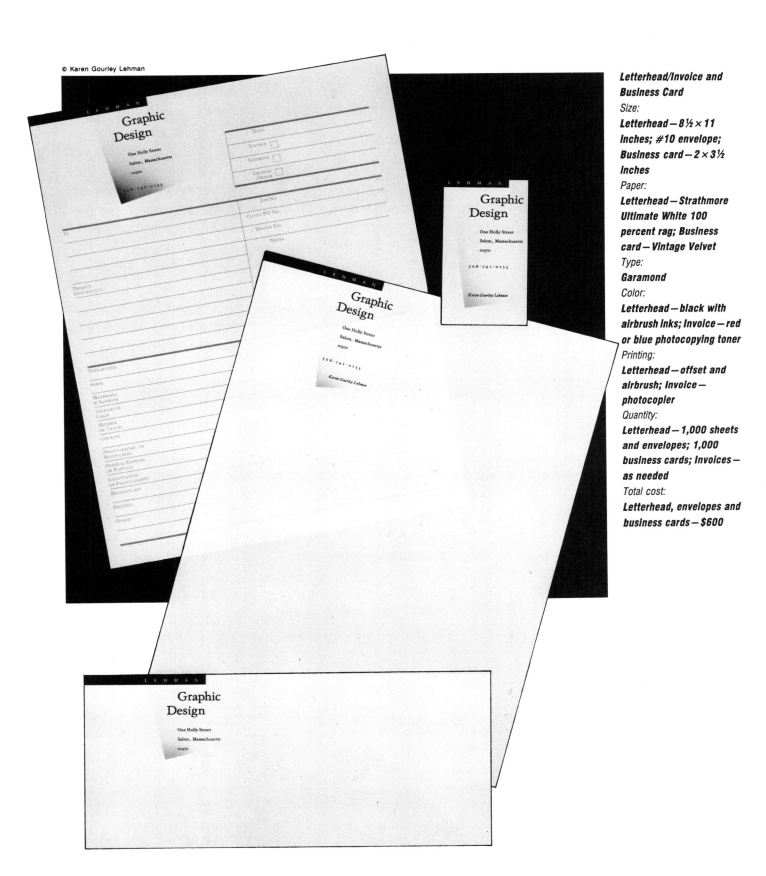

© Karen Gourley Lehman

Letterhead/Invoice and Business Card

Size:
Letterhead — 8½ × 11 inches; #10 envelope; Business card — 2 × 3½ inches

Paper:
Letterhead — Strathmore Ultimate White 100 percent rag; Business card — Vintage Velvet

Type:
Garamond

Color:
Letterhead — black with airbrush inks; Invoice — red or blue photocopying toner

Printing:
Letterhead — offset and airbrush; Invoice — photocopier

Quantity:
Letterhead — 1,000 sheets and envelopes; 1,000 business cards; Invoices — as needed

Total cost:
Letterhead, envelopes and business cards — $600

Pressing Self-Promotion

Jennifer Kennard
Kennard Design
Seattle, Washington

A "hands-on" designer who applauds simplicity and low-tech processes, Jennifer Kennard marries illustration with design, owns her own letterpress, and has been known to take a product all the way from the drawing table through final printing herself.

Kennard exudes an "I can do that" attitude growing out of, perhaps, her entry into the design field. She started working in 1978 "originally doing a lot of production" in advertising agencies but notes that much of what she learned was self-taught. "I started freelancing and it was a learning experience, on my own. People would come up to me and say they wanted something printed and I would have to find out how to do it."

Now serving a clientele composed primarily of wineries and a greeting card publisher, Kennard brings to her business the dual talents of illustration and design, offering clients an illustrative style that ranges from a detailed, fine art look to "the look of real rough imagery, either cut in linoleum or scratchboard." She considers her design skills stronger than her illustration but observes that the two fields overlap for her. Indeed, combining the two fields is "like taking the graphic design business and giving it a fine art edge."

She purchased a 1935 Kelsey 6 × 10 letterpress in 1990 to enhance her production capabilities and add yet another dimension to her diversity. "I've always loved printing and getting involved. I've done a lot of linoleum block, which ties in with letterpress on a very basic level." Both processes involve "applying ink to a raised surface and then printing it on paper." The result is "a quality that you can't find in offset printing."

The letterpress offered a unique approach to her yearly Christmas card, her self-promotion piece that boasts a nearly fifteen-year tradition. With this new tool, she created her Faux Snow greeting, one of her most popular cards.

"The Faux Snow Christmas card was produced as a gesture of gratitude for personal friends and business clients. It developed after an idea I had to do a "faux snow" concept with a silkscreen pattern. After inquiring about printing estimates, it wasn't long before I was back at the drawing board to design a new method of production. Silkscreen was prohibitive considering the small volume; offset was out of the question; so I began to consider stencil painting them individually and letterpress printing one color, both sides," Kennard explains.

The front of each card was "hand painted with the aid of a stencil, acrylic paint, sponges and a toothbrush. No two Faux Snow cards are alike." The inside message and the back of the card were executed on the letterpress.

Although "this provided me with the perfect opportunity to promote the usefulness of my letterpress," the process was a learning experience and not without its problems. "After many trials at setting the type properly, adjusting and registering the paper, the press was finally ready to go. Unfortunately, the temperature outside had been steadily below freezing for days and this affected the printability of the ink. So with one person on the press and another holding a heat gun on the ink at varying intervals, we managed to turn out about one hundred twenty-five cards total.

"The faux snow was packaged into small zip-lock bags and attached with a glue strip to the front of each card. Aside from the envelopes to mail them, the snow and zip-lock bags were the only outside costs. The beautiful Rives heavyweight paper had been donated on a previous job I worked on and this was the remainder of it. Although the actual production of this Faux Snow promo proved to be a comedy of errors, the very favorable response the cards have received has

© 1990 Jennifer Kennard

FAUX SNOW

HAVE A VERY
HAPPY HOLIDAY
AND AN UNREAL
NEW YEAR

THE ALL-BUBBA PRESS

"Let's Put the X Back in Xmas"

IN THE SPIRIT OF XMAS,
THIS INAUGURAL PRINTING WAS
PRODUCED ON DECEMBER 21ST, 1990
ON A RECENTLY ACQUIRED 1935
KELSEY 6X10 LETTERPRESS,
LOCATED INSIDE A COLD BASEMENT
OVERLOOKING A STEEP RAVINE
WITH 10 INCHES OF ICE & SNOW,
IN SEATTLE, WASHINGTON,
47 DEGREES NORTH AND
2 DEGREES CENTIGRADE.

WE HAD NOTHING BETTER TO DO.

Faux Snow Card
Size:
6⅜ × 4⅝ inches
Paper:
Rives Heavyweight Buff
Type:
Spartan, Modern Bodoni,
Futura Extra Bold, Caslon
Color:
Custom mixed
Printing:
Front—hand painted;
Inside and back—
letterpress
Quantity:
125
Unit cost:
28 cents
Distribution:
By mail
Mailing:
First class

been its own reward."

Kennard's innovation and creative design for self-promotion materials began long before the purchase of her letterpress, however. In 1987, a move from Los Angeles to Seattle found Kennard re-entering the job market seeking a staff position; this precipitated the need for "cheap, quick and unusual" self-promotion materials and the creation of the 5½ × 7⁵⁄₁₆-inch A R T envelope. Designed to hold samples of her work, "which are small because most are wine labels and greeting cards," the A R T envelope was a unique method of keeping the samples together and showing another example of her talent. The envelope and its samples were mailed out with a cover letter inside another envelope.

> **Unsuspecting is often the most interesting. Sometimes the most unusual objects can become the most interesting promotion pieces.**

The design on the front of the A R T envelope was originally created as a self-promotion poster idea for which Kennard combined visuals from her files and old magazines. The images were enlarged and manipulated by photocopying until the ties spelled ART and were being hung on a clothesline by a woman. For the envelope, Kennard reduced the poster image and photocopied it onto the envelope's front. Kennard also inexpensively constructed the envelope itself with "kraft-like and scrap papers" and even in some cases she "just tore apart some shopping bags."

Kennard received a response from all twenty-five potential employers she contacted. The interview process, however, brought home to Kennard the realization that she didn't want to work as an employee, and she's been freelancing since.

Though she no longer needs to do a great deal of self-promotion to obtain clients, Kennard sometimes does specialty mailings and "will continue to do them. They aren't really promoting my business, but are more to keep my name out there so people don't forget who I am. I work out of my house, and I don't want to lose touch with the design community."

Her overall view of self-promotion is "to keep it simple and make it something that you would like to receive in the mail yourself. Look at alternative printing processes and materials. There is no reason you can't take a sponge off your kitchen sink and turn that into a promotion piece somehow. Just take everyday materials and evolve them into something that can be a lot of fun.

"Unsuspecting is often the most interesting. Sometimes the most unusual objects can become the most interesting promotion pieces. Have a sense of humor. People like to get anything that is whimsical and humorous—those are remembered far longer than others because people keep them."

A R T Envelope
Size:
5½ × 7⁵⁄₁₆ inches
Paper:
Kraft, scrap, paper bags
Type:
None
Color:
Black toner
Printing:
Photocopier
Quantity:
25 and as needed
Unit cost:
None
Distribution:
Mailed inside another envelope
Mailing:
First class

Another Great Idea

Carmen Ramírez
AGI graphics
Tampa, Florida

After graduating from the University of South Florida in 1988, it didn't take Carmen Ramírez long to quit her part-time studio job and go solo. AGI graphics came into its own that summer. "While I was going to school, I worked part-time, but my husband and I had a computer at home that I used to do freelance jobs. He was encouraging me to do it on my own and at the time he was going to school in advertising also. We started doing more and more freelance work, and I decided to leave my studio job and head out on my own." Ramírez's husband, Roberto D. Colón, is her partner in the graphic services firm, which specializes in print, such as ads, brochures and logos.

The decision was a good one. "We are really happy. We had the office at our home for two years and moved to a new office in May of 1990. It's been going great since then." One of the best self-promotions the firm did, according to Ramírez, was to hold an open house to celebrate its new office space. "We sent out an invitation to nearly everybody in town, and people were able to come in and meet us and see our equipment. It was a good self-promotion because we got a lot of new clients and new business."

The other main self-promotion effort of the firm has been printed pieces. First was the pyramid (shown opposite), a glossy, full-color piece with three triangular sides, designed so that each triangle folds closed onto a triangular base to create a final ten-inch triangular package. When unfolded, the points and base combine to create an 8¾-inch-high pyramid. When the piece was created, "we had a third person working with us, Laurel Rummel. She suggested the idea because it was different, it represented the three of us, and could communicate the power of three and the

power of the pyramid." Though Rummel is no longer with the firm, the piece is still used as the company's brochure. Postal regulations prevent mailing the pyramid without an envelope, so it is handed out at personal reviews or put into a package of materials a potential client might request. It presents a visual message on the inside by presenting some of the firm's products in black-and-white as well as written text that wraps up with "You Want AGI." The cost per piece was low, $1.50, due to a trade-off with the printer. "We did some designing for him, and he in turn printed that piece for us."

The second piece (page 43) was created specifically to be a self-mailer, so Ramírez went to the post office first to learn what can and can't be mailed without an envelope. After settling on a 5½ × 6-inch bifold, costs were kept down by using one-color printing. Different screens of the color and reverse color printing add visual interest and

© 1991 AGI graphics

Pyramid Promotion

Size:

Closed — 10-inch triangle;
Open — pyramid 8¾ inches
high on 10-inch base

Paper:

Kromecote C2S 10 point

Type:

Helvetica Black

Color:

Full-color

Printing:

Offset

Quantity:

3,000

Unit cost:

$1.50 plus trade-off

Distribution:

Handed out and mailed
with samples

Mailing:

First class

the feeling of two-color. The cover features a man carrying a portfolio case, die-cut to open and show the letters AGI, and brief written text. The text is printed on a translucent paper insert that appears paper-clipped to the inside of the folder, but is actually held in place with light adhesive. Cost for each piece was fifty cents plus fifteen cents postage. Mailed recently, assessment of its success is difficult, although Ramírez notes that "we have already had five or six calls and it's only been a month. And we're going to do follow-up calls because this is the time of year that people are back from vacations and start their advertising after summer."

Ramírez also believes in what she calls "indirect self-promotion — the service you give the clients. Because of good service and treating your clients right, you get a lot of referrals. That's how we've been able to grow so fast. Do it right and in turn people are going to hear about you."

Finally, the burning question: What does AGI stand for? Ramírez laughs when she explains that in the beginning it stood for "A Graphic Impression. But that name was too long and people just started to call it AGI, which really sticks in people's minds because it's short. So we just make up new things that it can stand for and right now we say it's Another Great Idea."

© 1991 AGI graphics

Die-cut Portfolio
Size:
5½ × 6 Inches
Paper:
Concept by Beckett 80-pound Sand
Type:
Avant Garde
Color:
Purple PMS 275
Printing:
Offset
Quantity:
2,000
Unit cost:
50 cents
Distribution:
Malled
Mailing:
Bulk — 15 cents

An Idea Worth Keeping

**John Bielenberg
Marks/Bielenberg Design
San Francisco, California**

A sense of experimentation and the desire to do a unique self-promotion led John Bielenberg and fellow senior designers Allen Ashton and Brian Boran to create a brochure that seems to break all the rules. Not only is it tabloid size, but the firm's "You Can't Throw Away an Idea" brochure is printed in one color.

Bielenberg wanted a piece to reflect the thinking — the philosophy and the approach — that goes on behind design projects. The form of this promotion needed to reflect *concept* rather than be just another highly produced or colorful piece. Producing it cheaply in one color on recycled paper was in line with the designers' goal that the promotion be true to form and concept. They were also interested to see "if a design firm could do something that was really inexpensive and still get people interested in seeing the portfolio."

The piece attracted potential clients, small and large. "I've had calls from Apple Computer, Hewlett-Packard, and Pacific Gas and Electric," Bielenberg states. "It seemed to appeal to and elicit interest from different kinds of firms. For the dollars spent, the value was really high because a lot of people were intrigued by this brochure even though it was somewhat raw and different."

The 17½ × 11½-inch tabloid size was selected because — "with just one color and cheap paper, we felt we needed scale to give it any kind of presence. Also we were trying to make it as efficient as possible to print. We were working with a web printer and this tabloid size happens to be quite efficient" for that type of press.

The simplicity of the project and the use of efficient web printing was a pleasant change for Bielenberg. "It was fun because it was so direct. We produced the piece on the computer in one day,

got Linotronic copy, pasted it down, and it was to the printer on a Friday. The following Wednesday he was delivering the brochures to us. That was refreshing because most projects take months — this was more direct in its communication." The cost to produce 2,500 copies of the sixteen-page brochure was under $1,000.

Strong graphics, created to look like hand-drawn black arrows, guide the recipient through the brochure. Strategically placed bold type creates the scant text; it also lists the small firm's creative products, clients and awards. The theme of the brochure focuses on the client and firm working together to discover and develop objectives to drive the design "resulting in a solution that doesn't depend on preconceived notions of style or techniques and that compellingly conveys an idea." An idea that remains "long after the item itself is gone. Because . . . You can't throw away an idea."

The brochure was mailed out and is a major component of portfolio reviews where Bielenberg walks the client through it "emphasizing the way we work in developing objectives. When you're talking to primarily businesspeople, they're not that interested in the latest design style or the way you finesse typography. What presses their buttons has to do with goals and objectives."

When creating self-promotion pieces, Bielenberg advises to "make sure there is a real concept and a real understanding of what you're trying to do and who the audience is for the piece. Ideas can work much better than something that is slickly produced and colorful, but similar to other pieces. There is so much printed communication today that color and production are standard — they're not special. Concept and ideas are so much more important now than lavish production. So if you don't have enough money to do some slick piece, I don't think it's a hindrance at all if you approach it right."

© Marks/Bielenberg Design

You can't

throw

away

an

idea

Annual Reports
Brochures
Corporate Identity
Environmental Graphics
Exhibits
Logos
Packaging
Posters
Products
Signage

Marks/Bielenberg believes that graphic design is a thoughtful and creative process.

A process that includes working with the client to discover and develop strategic objectives.

These objectives then drive the design, resulting in a solution that doesn't depend on preconceived notions of style or technique and compellingly conveys an idea.

An idea that remains long after the item itself is gone. Because...

...you can't throw away an idea.

CLIENT ← → MARKS/ BIELENBERG

OBJECTIVES

DESIGN

IDEA

Marks/Bielenberg's work is included in the permanent collection of the Library of Congress and has been recognized with over 75 communication and design awards including:

For a portfolio review contact John Bielenberg at 415 495-3371

"You Can't Throw Away an Idea" Brochure
Size:
**17½ × 11½-inch tabloid;
16 pages**
Paper:
Simpson Offset Recycled
Type:
**Univers 55, Univers 65,
Univers 75**
Color:
Black
Printing:
Web press
Quantity:
2,500
Unit cost:
Approximately 40 cents
Distribution:
Mailed and handed out
Mailing:
First class

A Team by Design

**Sheree Clark and John Sayles,
Partners
Sayles Graphic Design
Des Moines, Iowa**

When a "right brainer" meets a "left brainer" the outcome can be a mutually beneficial creative partnership. That's what happened for John Sayles and Sheree Clark, the working partners who formed Sayles Graphic Design in 1985. The pair met when Clark was an administrator at Drake University in Des Moines and Sayles was a freelancer working for the university. Eventually the two formed a business. "As a freelancer, I was frustrated by having to do everything myself," recalls Sayles. "I'm best at, and happiest, being on the board. Client meetings, billings, scheduling— all those things took me away from what I knew I should be doing." For Clark, on the other hand, those things were right up her professional alley, and she adds that "John and I are a good balance for each other. I *like* left-brain activities! Also, because I'm not a designer, we're able to avoid some of the conflicts that occur when both principals have design backgrounds."

The staff of Sayles Graphic Design currently includes one other full-time designer and two part-time student interns. Its clients are nationwide and in all areas of business. "Our favorite work is that where we can have some fun," states Clark. "Sure we can do 'corporate' design, but we really shine when we're asked to do something attention-getting."

The firm's ability to create attention-getting materials doesn't stop with its clients; it extends to its self-promotion materials as well. Sayles insightfully observes that "our notion of what self-promotion is has changed over time. When we first started our business we were 'looking for work.' We found projects through traditional sales efforts. Sheree called on potential clients, sent letters and

samples, etc. While we still do some of these things, now we're actually looking for business relationships. We want to work *with*—as opposed to *for*—people and companies that view us and our work in a certain way. Frankly, there are people who we won't work with again because their philosophies don't mesh with ours."

One occasion that combines having a good time with self-promotion every year is the firm's party to celebrate the local Addy awards presentation. The invitations are creative, low-cost and memorable.

The invitation mailed in January 1991 combined the announcement of the party with a thank you for the previous year's business and friendship. Stock corrugated cardboard boxes were purchased locally for less than fifty cents each and customized with the firm's colors through the use of adhesive-back "labels" that were printed by piggybacking to a client's job. The top label states that the box holds a "Token of Our Appreciation" and inside is a foil-wrapped chocolate "token" imprinted with the Sayles logo. "The major cost was the candy, but now we have the die to use again later," Clark states. Even with the cost of the die and the chocolate, the unit cost was less than three dollars a piece.

The staff hand assembled the four hundred invitations during the weekend; they were mailed to out-of-town clients and hand delivered locally. The invitation was a successful method of keeping the Sayles name in front of current and potential clients. "Although the chocolate tokens are long gone, I still go into offices and see that people have kept their invitations," Clark notes.

For its "Let Us Wine and Dine You" invitation to celebrate the Addy awards, the firm purchased stock jewelry boxes from a packaging supplier. Silver-plated forks were purchased at local antique stores with a self-imposed $1.50 limit set for each. Corks were supplied by a restaurant-client

Token of Appreciation Invitation

Size:
Box—5½ × 5½ × 2 inches; Token—3-inch diameter

Paper:
Outside—Mactac "Starliner"; Inside—gloss enamel stock; Token—red foil

Type:
Futura Bold

Color:
Outside—red, gold, black; Inside—black

Printing:
Outside—offset; Inside—photocopied

Quantity:
400

Unit cost:
Less than $3

Distribution:
Mailed and handed out

Mailing:
First class

Wine and Dine Invitation
Size:
8 × 2 × 1 inches
Paper:
Inside—French Paper
Speckletone Cream; Inside
backing—red pebble
board
Type:
Futura Black
Color:
Black
Printing:
Offset
Quantity:
200
Unit cost:
$2.50
Distribution:
Mailed in padded envelope
and handed out
Mailing:
First class

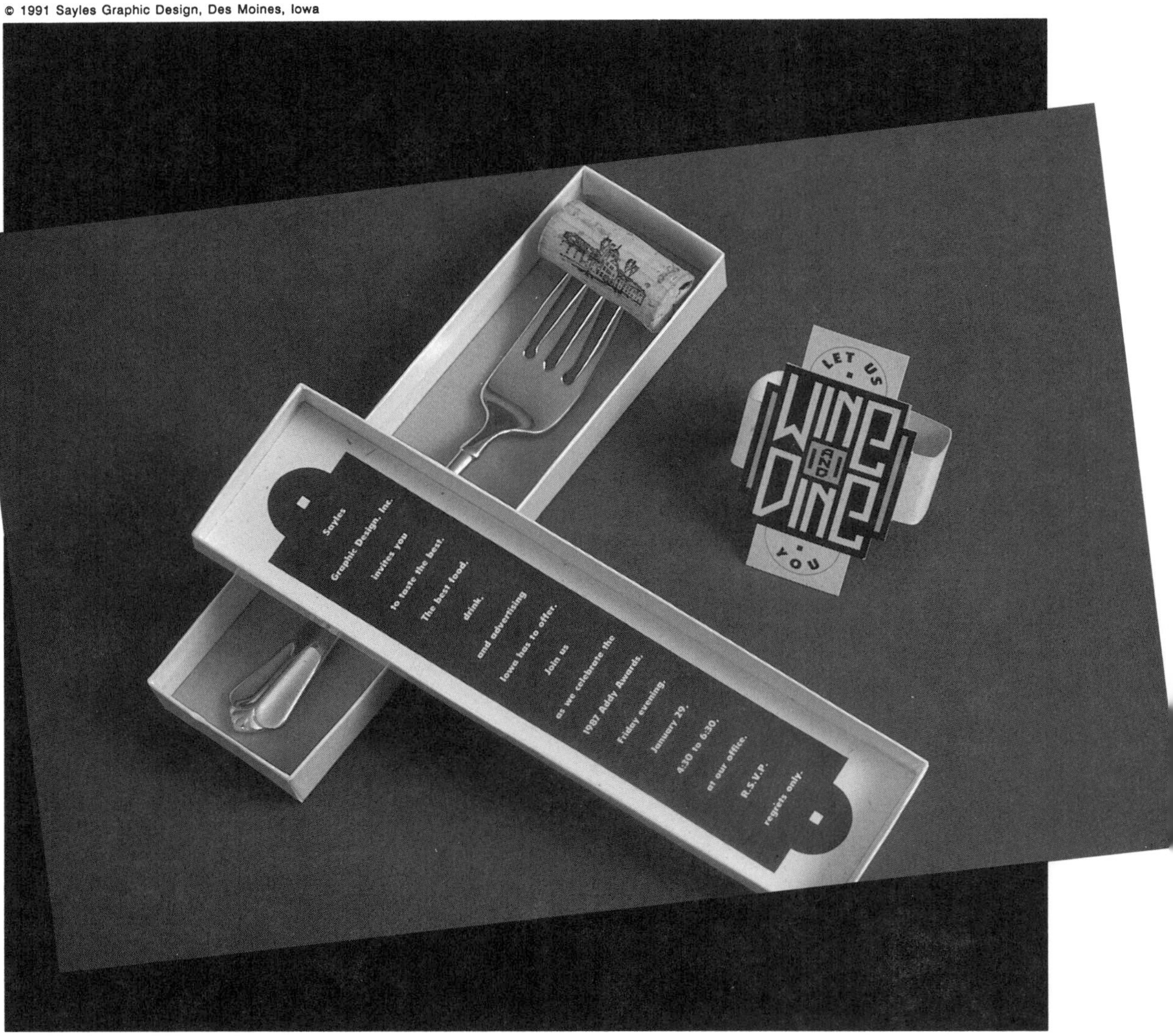

and red pebble board was placed on the bottom of each box to serve as a backdrop. The printed portion of the invitation was one color and the staff assembled the invitations. It went over so well that a few people even asked if they should bring the forks to the party.

As a business, Sayles Graphic Design is high on team effort and communicates this sense of corporate togetherness through indirect self-promotion—one that isn't geared to a specific

> **Remember the importance of follow-up. A one-shot effort isn't effective.**

clientele and is consciously limited in its distribution. Staff jackets bearing the colorful business logo are the pride of the Sayles Graphic Design team. The idea for the jackets developed during a staff meeting. "We were talking about some sportswear we had designed for a client when someone said, wouldn't it be cool if we had our own sweatshirts? That idea evolved into the jackets." It was decided that each person would design his/her own jacket by specifying different colors for the sleeves and other jacket elements. Sayles Graphic Design paid for the large chenille loop patches for the jackets' backs, which cost

48

Sayles Graphic Design staff jackets.

approximately seventy dollars each, and each individual picked up the cost of the custom-designed jacket, about $130 each. "Although we can't actually trace new work or clients to them," Clark explains, "they've generated a great deal of response." When staff members wear the jackets out, people "come up to us and begin a conversation about the business or say they've heard of us. An added plus is what it does for staff morale. We have 'team pride' and it shows!" In fact, the jackets have become somewhat of a status symbol: "Clients and suppliers saw the jackets and asked about buying their own. We asked the staff what

they thought of the idea and they overwhelmingly said, no way—these are exclusively for staff." However, the firm does have black Sayles Graphic Design sweatshirts that it makes available to "outsiders."

As the firm continues to prosper, the partners pass along learned self-promotion advice. "Think like a client! Ask yourself what your objectives are. Awareness? New business? A way to say thank you? Weigh the cost of production (don't forget to factor in your time) against the possible outcomes. Remember the importance of follow-up. A one-shot effort isn't effective."

Where There's a Will . . .

Robert. B. Allen
Graphic Designer
Kansas City, Missouri

Undaunted is the only word to describe Robert Allen, a staff designer in Kansas City, Missouri. During his school days at Columbia College, Columbia, Missouri, and the University of Missouri, Kansas City, Allen experienced an internship, freelancing, and a series of low-paying jobs, but the main portion of his income was derived from waiting tables. Graduating in 1984, Allen searched for a full-time job as a designer, but continued freelancing, working temporary jobs and waiting tables. Finally Allen substituted for a month for vacationing designers at Montague-Sherry Advertising which, in 1988, led to a full-time position. "Then I was a real, live art director who stopped waiting tables," Allen chuckles. "Actually I did self-promotion to get that job. I sent materials in a couple of times, just samples of some of my printed freelance work, with a letter to the art director saying that I was very interested in either doing freelance work or working full-time. The last thing I did was a little mailer about eight pages long that talked about how hard it was to get a job these days. It was pretty comical with cartoons in it. I hand drew all of them, and airbrushed it, and went all out to make it a strong comp just as I would do for a client today. At the end was a little pop-up that said, 'I really want this job'." Not only did he get the job, but within nine months of his arrival at the agency, Allen was senior art director.

As an art director, Allen was responsible for hiring personnel, and he learned valuable lessons for his own future job-hunting. On the receiving end of numerous résumés, he became a stickler about the importance of a well-designed résumé. When hiring for Montague-Sherry, "we put an ad in the paper once and received résumés from that. People would actually write in magic marker on paper and send it in! We probably got fifty résumés, and there were maybe three that I thought were designed okay. Here the résumé was my first exposure to what they could do as designers and most didn't think it was that important. Some of them even went to the expense of having their résumés printed, and they still looked awful. If you're going to spend the money, why not take the time to do it right?"

The résumé became a focal point for Allen when a year and a half later he decided to move toward a studio atmosphere, because "I felt I wasn't getting enough design time and wasn't growing as a designer." The decision led to the creation of his own résumé, a piece whose design he vowed would not be missed in the mail. "It was going to blow everything else away," Allen states. He designed the business card and résumé simultaneously, each incorporating a diagonal and horizontal fold as an integral part of the design, a fold that turns the piece from horizontal to vertical as it's opened. "I have always liked this fold and thought that there had to be some way to make it work for me. I designed around the fold—when the résumé is closed it gives basic information on the front about my education and address and says, graphic design and art direction. Then it opens up to talk about my experience and more about me. I was very happy the way it all progressed."

Though intricate in appearance, the résumé cost next to nothing to produce. The sixty sheets of paper were a thank you from a sales rep; Allen created all of the artwork on the computer. Typesetters in his building were good friends who set the type for free. Allen did all of the keyline, and when he went to the camera shop, also in the building, the piece was shot in exchange for a couple of cases of beer. Now "I had all of the final film and the paper, so I was prepared to pay for the printing. There was a new printing shop just

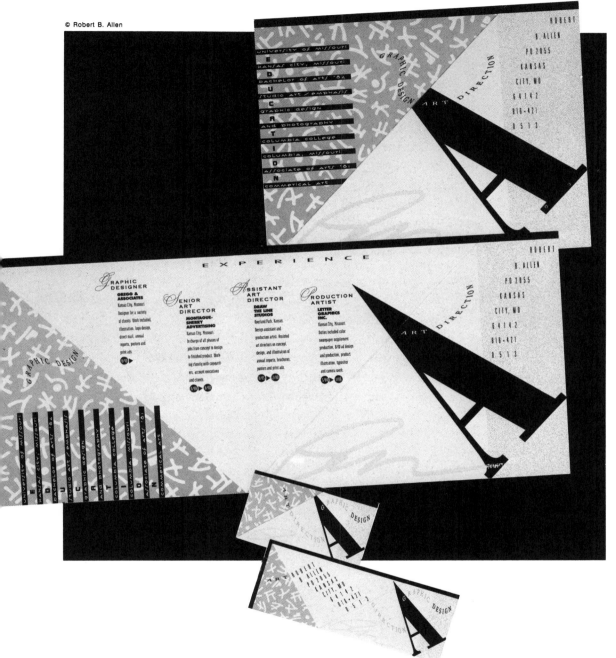

Résumé and Business Card

Size:

Résumé — closed 7 × 9 inches, open 7 × 16 inches; Business card — closed 2 × 3½ inches, open 2 × 5½ inches

Paper:

French Paper Tuscan Terra Flax

Type:

Modula Serif, Copperplate, Futura Extra Bold, Varix, Eurostyle, Univers 49, Mellor

Color:

Black, PMS blue

Printing:

Offset

Quantity:

60 sheets of cardstock

Total cost:

Two cases of beer and trade-offs

Distribution:

Mailed

Mailing:

First class

around the block that was more or less a quick-copy place, but since the résumé was just two colors, I thought they could handle it. The registration was tight, but because the printers were just starting out, I figured they'd be eager to please. They looked at it and said they'd like to do it in trade. So I ended up doing one piece for them in exchange for the printing." The final trimming and folding was done by hand by Allen.

The unfolded résumé is 7 × 16 inches, which allowed it to fit on an 11 × 17-inch sheet of card stock. "You don't see that many résumés on card stock and it's more durable." Allen used the extra sheet space to print his business card and a note card with part of the logo on it. Maximizing paper usage is one of Allen's guiding principles: "Find out how much space you've got on the sheet and use every single inch of it. You're going to be using that sheet size anyway." Within a week of sending the résumé out, Allen landed a job with Gregg & Associates where he works as a graphic designer.

His eye to a professional presentation also extends to a designer's portfolio. "I have reviewed a ton of portfolios and what I remember most strongly is that whenever photographers come in to show their work, it's always in a beautiful case, mounted well, and the transparencies always look great. Then I see people come in with their design portfolios and their work is just thrown in the case, flopping all around." Taking this lesson to heart, his own portfolio is in a case similar to the type photographers use. "Each piece is laminated on a board with information about who the client was, the project, and exactly what the piece is. If the reviewer feels like reading it, he can; if not, he can ignore it. I have the whole portfolio broken into sections—newspaper, magazine, brochures, and so on—and there is a little tag on each board that identifies it. In the front I have one big page that talks about my philosophy, which is that I don't

believe there is a huge gap between art directors and graphic designers. After all, if design is done right, it has content to it; if art direction is done right, it has design to it."

Another stumbling block to a smooth, professional presentation that Allen encountered was how to present his logos to clients who wanted to see only that specific material. With all of his logos mounted on one large board for his portfolio, Allen found it awkward to pull out and carry around to these clients and looked for a way to reduce its size yet give each logo equal emphasis. Solving this problem led to a pleasant, money-saving discovery in the form of a booklet that displays only his logos, icons and trademarks (shown on facing page).

Created primarily from scraps, the book first took shape when Allen photocopied his work onto gloss enamel stock. "Then I sprayed the photocopies with fixative, which melted the toner just enough to cover up any flaws and made the toner look 'blacker.' When the toner melted, it also raised off the paper, which gave it a feel similar to thermography. Then I sprayed that with a clear acrylic spray coating, which gave it a glossy, slick look. Everyone thinks it's been printed." Each "printed" logo was mounted onto heavier card stock and trimmed to 7¼ × 6½-inch pages. The pages were backed with blocks of colored Pantone paper, mostly leftover from other projects, which provided a splash of color. Allen designed the cover on the computer; following output on a laser printer, the cover was photostatted and mounted on heavy cardstock. The black plastic binding was put on at a print shop, where the booklet was punched and bound for about $1 to $1.50. The hard-edged, black-and-white cover not only coordinates well with the binding, but is representative of much of Allen's work.

Knowing that self-promotion is important, whether for a freelance business or to land a job,

LogoBook
Size:
7¼ × 6½ inches
Paper:
Leftover gloss enamel stock, cardstock, Pantone color blocks
Type:
Cover—self-designed; Individual logos—Futura Extra Black, Garamond Light Italic, and miscellaneous typeface
 Color:
Black photocopy toner
Printing:
Photocopying, laser printing, photostatting
Quantity:
Created as needed
Unit cost:
$1.00 to $1.50
Distribution:
Handed out

Allen strongly advocates that people who don't have a lot of money "find the resources around them, that are common to them, that they aren't even thinking about. Like using a photocopying machine and spraying with fixative so that a piece looks printed. Or find the things that you have left over in your studio and find ways to use them." If you don't have the money to do hundreds of pieces, then "target the piece you want to send" and do only the number of pieces you can afford. "Don't try to market to the world."

Promotions for Repeat Business

David Levy
David Levy Design, Inc.
Atlanta, Georgia

David Levy worked at an ad agency in Texas for a few years after finishing school, but in his heart he always knew he would always return to Atlanta, Georgia. When he did in the early '80s, he garnered experience that included working in a small studio, "which later became part of a much larger studio"; being creative director with a trade association, "which was good because it gave me the opportunity to run a studio"; and starting his own studio in partnership with a friend. The studio was a success but the partnership was not, and he left to open his own studio, David Levy Design, Inc., now three years old.

Building his company alone from the ground up, Levy explains how he went from a one-man operation with no clients to a firm that now employs two designers and a part-time administrative person. After leaving the partnership, "I called all of my vendors and let them know I would appreciate any leads they could give me. I didn't call the clients I had had because I really have a 'thing' about taking work away from other studios. I let people know I was leaving, but I didn't solicit their work directly. I let them know where they could find me if they wanted me."

Find him they did, but he admits that "it took time. It's taken about three years to develop stability with the cash flow and the client roster and to know that a few slow weeks are not a major cause for concern." Levy is optimistic about the growth of Atlanta, what with national and international corporations choosing it for headquarters and the Olympics arriving in 1996. When asked how he approaches these incoming firms, Levy explains that "my marketing approach is not super-aggressive. I know many studios try to get in as soon as a company arrives, but I try to wait until the air

clears. Sixty-five percent of my business is repeat. That's a huge amount, so I try to concentrate on staying in touch with and giving good service to the clients I have. Another twenty-five percent of my business is referral work from those clients or other people, and only ten percent is new business." Producing an excellent product is Levy's main goal because "your reputation certainly precedes you. If you do good work for a client, not only can he refer you to other people, but if he leaves and goes to work for another company, he will take you along to the new company. If you've done good work for others within the original company, you maintain them as a client. As long as you're doing good work and providing good service, you're way ahead of the game."

Hand-in-hand with this overall philosophy, Levy consistently keeps his studio's name in front of clients, prospects and peers through cost-effective, targeted mailings. When developing self-promotion pieces, "you have to have a great concept and design and it must be excellently produced. You can't fall down on the production because when someone receives it, that's his impression of you or your company. You have to use the production—how you're going to produce it—as a part of the design. You have to say, if silkscreening is the most cost-effective way to produce this piece, how can I incorporate that into the design to make it all work together?"

His six-inch square moving/expansion announcement (page 56) is an example of how Levy integrated the method of production and intended use for the piece into his overall design. Sent to clients, suppliers and friends, the card was printed on a cast-coated paper, metallic colored only on one side, which permitted the white back to be used for addressing. Levy purchased the paper direct from the merchant and saved the printer's markup. It was sent as a postcard to friends and vendors and inserted into an envelope for clients

Moving/Expansion
Announcement
Size:
6 × 6 inches
Paper:
Mohawk Splendorlux
Emerald
Type:
Futura Extra Bold
Color:
PMS 268 Purple
Printing:
Silkscreen
Quantity:
550
Unit cost:
$1.20
Distribution:
Mailed as self-mailers or in
envelopes
Mailing:
First class

and prospects because "it made a nicer presentation. There was no printing on the envelope, just the label." The piece was silkscreened because of the small run; nine cards were printed on each sheet of paper. The message announcing the studio's expansion to new space with the address is in the form of the company's logo and is the paper's metallic surface showing through the silkscreened background of matte purple ink. The layout and camera-ready art were prepared on a Macintosh computer. The total cost for the card including mailing was "less than one dollar twenty cents a piece for a quantity of five hundred fifty. I

have a very specific mailing list of about six hundred people that I update monthly. It's all on a database; vendors are categorized by type and clients are categorized by industry. Whenever I want to send a mailer just to my clients in the life insurance industry or just the paper industry, I can do that."

A 1990 holiday greeting card conveyed the theme of working together and that is exactly what Levy did — he and photographer Tommy Thompson collaborated on the project "so that each of our skills would be represented and costs shared." The studio tries to do a holiday card ev-

Piece: © 1990 David Levy Design, Inc.
Photography: © 1990 Tommy Thompson

Holiday Card
Size:
5 × 7 inches
Paper:
Simpson Evergreen Cover
Weight, Almond
(photograph) and Spruce
(card)
Type:
Bodoni Bold Expanded
Color:
Black
Printing:
Offset and Polaroid
photography
Quantity:
300
Unit cost:
$2.20 including postage
Distribution:
Mailed in envelope
Mailing:
First class

ery year, and "the important thing is to come up with something that makes sense as a card and yet is different." Again, purchasing the paper direct from the merchant and printing on one side were cost-cutting measures. Copy was written in-house and the layout and camera-ready art prepared on the Macintosh. The two men were able to combine mailing lists, weeding out duplicate names. The unusual photographic process allowed each card to possess its own nuances because each was created individually. A Polaroid photograph of the image is shot, but rather than allow the backing to transfer the image onto the

photographic paper, the backing is pulled off and the image is transferred directly onto fiber paper. "We produced a limited edition of three hundred," Levy states, "and film was our main cost." The image was dry mounted onto the pre-printed cover-weight card; families helped with this process. The greeting was put into standard-sized unprinted envelopes that matched the card; "the cost per piece including mailing was about two dollars and twenty cents. It was very effective for both of us, and we received a lot of response from it."

Remember the Big Picture

Kim Youngblood, President
Youngblood, Sweat & Tears
Atlanta, Georgia

Self-promotion for Youngblood, Sweat & Tears, the firm with the unforgettable name, encompasses community involvement, the environment, and winning design awards. "We consider promotion to include several different areas, the largest of which is public relations. We've produced a press kit. We have a whole public relations plan that I've developed over the years that maintains public speaking engagements and community service activities," states President Kim Youngblood.

As testimony to her design talent and community/environmental commitment, Youngblood has received two international Clios and more than fifty national and local creative awards. The listings on her bio sheet under affiliations/associations and activities/recognition categories fill an entire page. She has been a magazine contributing editor, speaker, panelist, competition judge, and Small Business Person of the Year finalist, to name only a few of her achievements.

For YS&T, founded in 1985, a strong stand on environmental issues is also "a very big part of our positioning," states Youngblood. "What is a promotion plan if you don't have a strong position? You have to give your target audience, your potential clients, a reason to choose you over somebody else." This commitment to the environment has placed the studio at the forefront of using only recycled paper or 100 percent cotton paper and promoting the recyclying of used paper. In fact its corporate commitment extends to its clients—all client work is produced on recycled paper. The firm accepts only new clients who have a commitment to the environment; it has even drawn up a corporate policy statement that lists its environmentally sound practices. Youngblood states that

"the main thing is to support the environment and to watch how much paper we turn out. Graphic designers have a great opportunity to create a demand for recycled paper and to have an impact on what the paper companies produce."

The 1990 YS&T Christmas promotion piece shown here was created because "we wanted to do a card for our clients and we wanted something that was relevant to recessionary times." Working from the firm's philosophy of "developing creative pieces that engage the mind as well as the eye," the "card" is a box that acknowledges that many agencies are cutting overhead. It intrigues the reader to find out how YS&T is adding to theirs. The clever answer is with mistletoe, of course.

Extremely low-cost, the greeting was produced entirely in-house. Only twenty were assembled because the mailing list targeted a select group of clients. Boxes were purchased for eighty-nine cents each, headlines were photocopied and hand glued to the box tops, and a sample sprig of artificial mistletoe was given by a local florist. Actually, the fact that it was artificial was a point of concern. "We like to do things impeccably, which meant using something that was real as opposed to fake. But as soon as we chopped real mistletoe from the stem, it tended to fade very quickly." Rather than have clients receive a shriveled sprig, the studio decided to use the artificial version.

1990 Box With Mistletoe
Size:
7¼ × 5¾ × 1 inches
Paper:
20-pound White
Type:
Goudy Bold
Color:
Black
Printing:
Photocopier
Quantity:
20
Unit cost:
89 cents
Distribution:
Mailed
Mailing:
First class

The select mailing list included fifteen ongoing client relationships as well as a few new business prospects, one of which was an international leather tannery. Youngblood notes that "I chased that piece of business for over a year. I sent letters and promotions and kept in touch." After receiving the card, a company representative "called and said, 'I love this Christmas card.' She gave us a piece of business just because of that card." For a promotion whose total production cost was under twenty dollars, the campaign more than paid for itself with just that one "piece of business."

Tying together her self-promotion and design philosophies, Youngblood advises that "all self-promotion efforts have to relate to one big picture, have to relate back to a plan. It's imperative to know who you are and what you want to accomplish. You can do the most creative thing in the world and if it gets attention, that's great, but if it reinforces the wrong message, then it's all for naught. If we were to send something out that was really neat looking, but looked like the typical graphic design piece, it would completely undermine all of our previous efforts introducing ourselves as a strategic design firm."

Promotion That's in the Bag

Tom Graham
TD Graham & Associates
Kemptville, Ontario

Tom Graham's background laid the perfect groundwork for his business, which he describes as "a combination of design, artwork production, consulting, and marketing communications development." During college he held part-time jobs in retailing, sales and business marketing. After graduating with a fine arts degree, a variety of experiences increased his firsthand knowledge of all aspects of business operation and promotion— owning his own retail business, designing and selling newspaper advertising, and working for an advertising agency that offered exposure to all media. He started his own firm, TD Graham & Associates, in October 1989, bringing to it the diverse background that enables him to relate easily to his clients.

Graham also teaches marketing for small businesses at a local community college, and not only shares commonsense self-promotion advice with his classes, but also uses it within his own business. "Self-promotion never stops," he states. "You answer the phone wrong and you're failing at self-promotion. Marketing goes on in your sleep because the letter that you send out is working for you while you are not making phone calls. To me self-promotion is like treading water—you can't stop. If you're in the water, you tread water or swim, but you cannot stop because you will sink."

> *To me self-promotion is like treading water—you can't stop. If you're in the water, you tread water or swim, but you cannot stop because you will sink.*

Graham advocates using press releases for "anything that happens, such as taking on a new project or hiring new staff. It's worth sending a note to the local paper or to the business press. If they run it, it's cheap advertising.

He also faithfully reads the business press and, if an article has particular application to his business, he sends it out to his clientele with a letter. For example, "I read where a consulting firm said that in time of recession a lot of companies can't afford to have high-priced overhead like marketing departments. It's cheaper to buy those services than to keep somebody on board full-time. I photocopied the article and excerpted the part that says what a good idea it is to hire outside services for specialized business needs. In my letter I point out the relevance to the graphic design business. Why have a full-time designer on staff if you don't have full-time design needs? I send this sort of thing out to both prospective and past clients. It doesn't necessarily generate calls right away, but I know they are thinking about me, and I know they're getting something with my name on it. Later it can lead to repeat business."

These low-cost techniques provide one of the most important ingredients to self-promotion: communication. As Graham quickly points out, "Communicate with both prospective *and* past customers. If you can keep past customers happy,

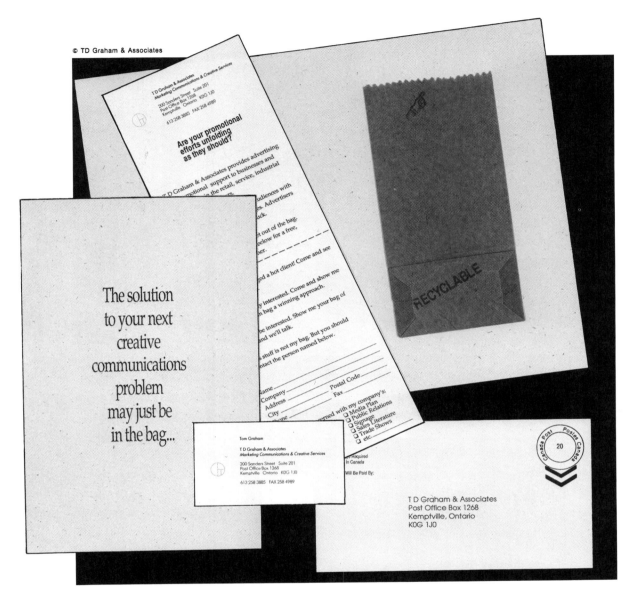

© TD Graham & Associates

The solution to your next creative communications problem may just be in the bag...

Tom Graham

T D Graham & Associates
Marketing Communications & Creative Services

200 Sanders Street   Suite 201
Post Office Box 1268
Kemptville Ontario   K0G 1J0

613 258 3885   FAX 258 4989

T D Graham & Associates
Post Office Box 1268
Kemptville, Ontario
K0G 1J0

Bag Mailer

Size:

Outside bag—12½ × 6⅛ inches; Bifold card—8½ × 5½ inches; Inside bag—6 × 3 inches; Folded promotion sheet—10¼ × 3 inches; Business card—2 × 3½ inches; Return envelope #8—3⅝ × 6½ inches

Paper:

Bifold card—Mayfair Cover; Folded promotion sheet—Letterhead on Gilbert Wove 24-pound Text Weight; Business card—Gilbert Wove Cover Weight

Type:

Palatino, Palatino Condensed, Helvetica Narrow

Color:

Black

Printing:

Bifold card—photocopier; Folded promotion sheet—laser printer; Envelope #8—offset

Quantity:

50

Unit cost:

$1.90 including postage

Distribution:

Mailed

Mailing:

First class

coming back for repeat business and referring other customers to you, that's where your business should come from."

When Graham first started his business he looked for a low-budget way to create impact and to increase awareness of his firm. The result was his "bag mailer," a 5½ × 8½-inch bifold card that arrives inside an ordinary 12½ × 6⅛-inch brown paper lunch bag. The card states on the front that "The solution to your next creative communications problem may just be in the bag . . . " and opens to display a small 6 × 3-inch brown paper bag glued to the inside. Graham explains that "the bag transcends the play on words and becomes an audience participation mechanism. The outer bag sets the stage for the inner piece." The inner bag holds a folded 10¼ × 3-inch promotional sheet with the lower half to be filled out and returned as a response card; a postage paid return envelope and business card are also included.

Fifty mailers cost approximately ninety-four dollars. "I paid one dollar for all of the bags and fifteen dollars to have my laser-printed type photocopied onto heavy cardstock. The postage on each was fifty-five cents. The rest was gluing, which was done by hand." The promotional insert was laser printed directly onto Graham's letterhead and then cut down to size so that his logo, name and address appear at the top. "It looks like a specially printed and folded form along with the business card and business reply envelope"; the envelopes were offset printed at a cost of fifty dollars for five hundred.

Graham compiled his mailing list from a directory of industries available at the library, past contacts, and people he wanted to do business with. The project was a success even though "nobody sent back the postage-paid business reply. However, when I did follow-up calls, the client would say, it looks great, I have it right here on my desk. When can you come and see me? I got that re-sponse from the first six people I called and I never got around to calling anybody else because I was catapulted into a flurry of projects." Though surprised that no one returned the response card, Graham believes using that approach made him appear organized and credible, and prefers to think of his response rate as 100 percent because "I got jobs from the first six people I called."

Graham's next promotion is a pop-up designed "while doodling in the solitude of my car between meetings." A recently designed pop-up wine invitation for a client had worked well and he became stuck on the idea of a pop-up for himself. Illustrator Linda Myers created the original caricature of Graham holding a removable business card. The type was set on his Macintosh computer and output to a laser printer; then the type and illustration were photocopied onto cardstock. The cutting and assembly of the pop-up caricature is done by hand with the inside construction glued to heavier textured cover stock. "They take about half an hour to put together. I have the raw materials to make up about fifty," which Graham considers to be manageable for in-house assembly.

Cost is estimated at under one dollar a piece including envelopes. Graham points out that "It's all small ingredients. You go to the photocopier and pay ten to twenty cents for each sheet of your cardstock. The cover stock is expensive, two to three dollars a sheet, but you get five or six cards out of it. So it's all small stuff." When a quiet day comes along the project will be completed; meanwhile the outlook for the piece is good because "clients and suppliers who come to my office get a real kick out of the one hanging on the wall."

© TD Graham & Associates

Why not call someone who stands out from the crowd?

Tom Graham

T D Graham & Associates
Marketing Communications & Creative Services

200 Sanders Street Suite 201
Post Office Box 1268
Kemptville Ontario K0G 1J0

613 258 3885 FAX 258 4989

FOR A NEW APPROACH
TO YOUR BUSINESS
COMMUNICATIONS..

Because you never know
when the need for effective
communications solutions
may pop up!

For outstanding creative
Advertising   Graphic Design
Illustration   Corporate Identity
Public Relations
Promotional Material

Call (613) 258-3885.
TD Graham & Associates

Pop-up
Size:
Closed — 8½ × 5½ inches;
Open — 17 × 5½ inches;
Business card — 2 × 3½
inches
Paper:
Cover — Canson mi-
Teintes; Inside — 200 M
Plainfield
Type:
Palatino Condensed
Color:
Outside — silver pen ink;
Inside — black
Printing:
Outside — by hand;
Inside — photocopier
Quantity:
50
Unit cost:
Approximately $1
Distribution:
Anticipated by mail
Mailing:
First class

Production to the Max

Maxi Harper
Maxi Harper Graphics
San Bruno, California

To read the extensive list of products and services provided by Maxi Harper Graphics, you would expect a studio spilling over with designers and production people. But Maxi Harper Graphics is only one person—Maxi Harper herself—which then prompts the question: How does she accomplish so much by herself?

The "how" is answered through the strategic use of technology. Although many designers today use computers and laser printers to aid their design production, Harper planned early to be at least one step ahead of the crowd. From her first purchase of a photostat machine in 1978, she strived always to find the equipment that would enable her to maintain the quality of and the control over her product that she desired. The realization that computers were the way of the future prompted her to research and buy equipment that would interface with a computer system giving her computer capabilities and the ability to upgrade her existing equipment "by having front-end pieces." Years of negotiating, networking and trading in old pieces for new ones have created the full-service studio of today where she has "a Packard Bell computer that interfaces to a professional Compugraphic typesetter. It gives me all of the capabilities of the computer and all of the photographic quality and capability of the phototypesetter. So I'm getting all of the accuracy from one machine when it is interfaced and all of the programming of the other." Harper has run her own business for eight years providing everything from layout, design and illustration to typesetting, halftones and photostats. Her client list includes hospitals, radio stations, cable networks, photographers, industrial manufacturers and service companies.

Photographer: David Leach

Until recently Harper relied on word of mouth and portfolio reviews, handled either by herself, or by part-time sales representative and spouse, Dennis Leach, to obtain clients. Then she decided to design her own self-promotion pieces to see if the marketing-related advice she was giving clients really worked. "I read all of the stats to keep current on what's happening in marketing and how to reach people. I advise my clients when it's good to do direct mail and when it's good to do newspaper ads." To make sure she was selling her clients good information. Harper decided to experience marketing on her own budget.

For her promotion piece, budget was the primary design factor. Harper notes that she's aware that others in the art fields say that creativity comes first and everything else follows. But Harper points out that "there are times when I sit down and say that money is the 'designing' factor here. Then I work off that the best I can." Because she does her own production, Harper can integrate the design process with her knowledge of where costs can be cut during the production of the piece to achieve a quality piece within a specific budget.

One of Harper's promotions is a black-and-white matchbook, 4¼ × 5¼ inches when closed,

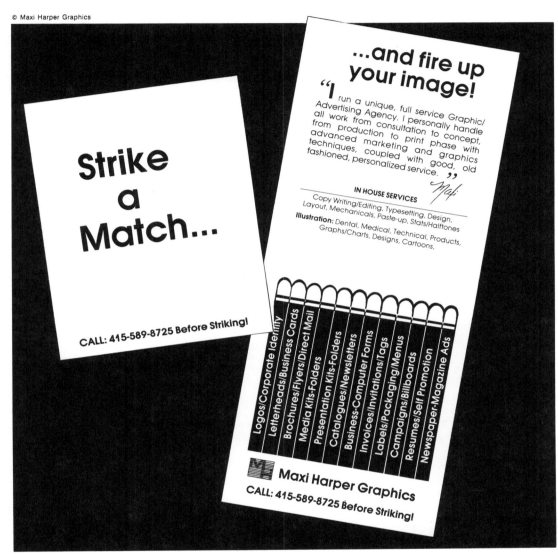

Matchbook

Size:
**Closed — 5¼ × 4¼ inches;
Open — 10 × 4¼ inches**

Paper:
Vellum Bristol White

Type:
Avant Garde Black

Color:
Black

Printing:
Offset

Quantity:
500

Unit cost:
24 cents

Distribution:
Mailed and handed out

Mailing:
First class

that urges potential clients to "Strike a match . . . and fire up your image." The printed "matches" inside describe her products and the individual sheets behind the matches show examples of her work. With in-house production, the cost to produce the matchbook was $120 for printing more than five hundred of the pieces. The printer cut and scored the pieces; Harper put the books together.

Targeted to promote her work primarily to retail and product development clients, the inexpensive matchbook has proven to be a hit with all types of potential clients. Harper states, "I went to a business party the other night and took some with me; yesterday the phone was ringing off the hook. People just love this piece." And business acquaintances aren't the only ones likely to receive one of Harper's matchbooks: "If someone at a cocktail party asks if I have a match, I give them a matchbook." The impact of the piece can also be measured by the fact that clients initially receiving the matchbook pass the promotion along to subsidiaries; Harper has reaped three business contacts from that alone and believes it will continue to escalate.

Harper's medical illustration sample sheet is targeted to clients within the medical, dental, athletic therapy and chiropractic professions and was designed to work most efficiently within the medical professional's system where "everything has to be in a file." Stapled into a labeled folder with a dossier, the samples are directed to the client's interests, and the entire piece is ready to go through the receptionist's hands directly to the appropriate desk "where it will be read because it is a file. They won't toss it aside or ask what they should do with it or say we have to make a folder for this—it's all ready to go." Harper has made a follow-up call as late as six months after sending the promotion and received the response, "Oh yes, I remember you; you're the one who was so nice to give us the folder." Another benefit to a folder presentation is that during a personal review if the client makes notes, "they can just stick them in the folder and everything's right there."

The folders themselves were the greatest expense for this piece because Harper produced the halftones for the medical illustrations and used her letterhead for both the sample sheet and dossier. For the sample sheet, it cost about fifty dollars for offset printing in black ink; when a sample sheet consists of line drawings, the cost is even less. Providing her own paper cuts down cost to the point where line drawings can be run through a quick printer for only about thirty dollars.

© Maxi Harper Graphics

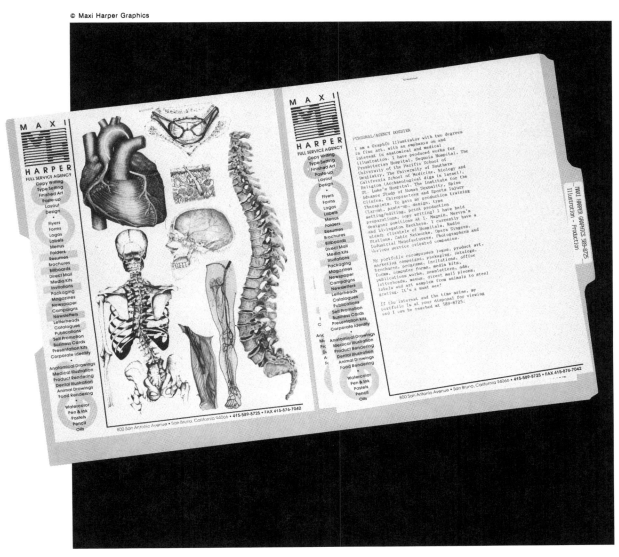

Medical Folder

Size:

**Illustration sheet —
8½ × 11 inches; Dossier —
8½ × 11 inches; Folder —
9½ × 11¾ inches**

Paper:

**Letterhead — Neenah
Classic Crest Gray; Gray
file folder**

Type:

Letterhead — Avant Garde

Color:

Black

Printing:

Offset

Quantity:

500

Unit cost:

53 cents

Distribution:

Mailed and handed out

Mailing:

First class

A Stand-Out Promotion

Robert Upton, Senior Designer
Designed Marketing
Minneapolis, Minnesota

Sometimes a designer just has to do what a designer has to do to make a self-promotion work. When the seven employees of Designed Marketing wanted a Christmas card that would stand out from the more traditional holiday greetings, Bob Upton came up with the idea of putting the card on a different type of surface. He opted for corrugated cardboard, inexpensive yet unusual for a holiday greeting, but he found out that when you deal with the post office you have to ask them about the postal regulations governing the practicalities of mailing your creation, and that usually "they'll say no, you can't or it won't work."

So Upton took the situation into his own hands and mailed himself pieces of cardboard of varying sizes and weights to find out what would and wouldn't go through the mail. To his delight, though he wouldn't speculate on what his mailman was beginning to think, all of the pieces were delivered with no problems. His Christmas card idea was one step closer to reality.

Measuring 4⁵⁄₁₆ × 5⅞ inches, the Christmas card is silkscreened in red, green and ivory on only one side and features the Foshay Tower in Minneapolis, a historic landmark filled with charm and style and in which the design firm is located. Upton chose silkscreen as the method of printing to give the piece more of a handmade and "less slick" look and hired a printer "who really doesn't work with design firms; he usually just prints logos on packing boxes." This was the ideal vendor for this type of card because he works with sheets of cardboard every day. "He was a different resource for us, but definitely within our ballpark budget."

Two hundred cards were printed; the final cost was approximately one dollar a piece.

To minimize pre-printing costs, Upton cut type out of a type book and photocopied artwork that was readily available because Upton is a collector of old postcards and brochures featuring the historic building. The paste-up was completed on a Macintosh computer. "There was a lot of hand work instead of jobbing things out. The piece came back from the printer untrimmed—it just had crop marks. We got the whole office together and spent an afternoon trimming them out. We also addressed the cards and put the postage on." Mailing the piece as a postcard saved the cost of an envelope.

As the firm's 1989 greeting, the holiday card was a definite success. Upton states, "A lot of people commented on that piece because it was so unusual at the time. I think other people have done similar things since then, but we received a lot of comments" about its uniqueness and originality. "It definitely stood out from the many generic cards they received during the holidays."

Upton notes that the firm tries to tie most of its promotions into an event. "It can be a holiday or a special occasion such as when we moved our office—we did quite a big promotion then." Upton advises that you use any reason to get your name out into the marketplace. He also admits that "I *like* to get little books and cards in the mail." At the design studio, Upton receives so many posters and highly produced pieces that "it's unique to get a piece that's a different size" or looks creatively low-cost.

Christmas Card
Size:
4⁵⁄₁₆ × 5⅞ inches
Paper:
⅛-inch corrugated cardboard
Type:
Futura, Hand drawn
Color:
Red, green, ivory
Printing:
Silkscreen
Quantity:
200
Unit cost:
$1
Distribution:
Mailed
Mailing:
First class

Hitting Your Niche

**Tom Scott
The Art of Business
West Conshohoken,
Pennsylvania**

The Art of Business is only six months old, but owner/designer Tom Scott states that "I seemed to hit a real niche at the right time." When he left his position as a senior art director at a Philadelphia ad agency to start his own marketing communications firm, Scott believed he would be employed by other agencies to act as a "hired gun" to work on special projects. Instead, he's delighted to find himself working directly with small- and medium-size companies as well as having the opportunity to work with several "start-up companies. I'm helping them develop the initial image and then working on everything—public relations, logos, direct mail campaigns and advertising. I try to think of cost-effective ways of promoting their businesses just as I try and do for mine."

Scott's letterhead system is just one of the ways he saves money within his own company. Designed in-house, the system is made of various components that can be mixed according to the intended use and to customize individual pieces. The components are: letterhead, second sheets, #10 envelopes, 9 × 12-inch envelopes, adhesive-back labels, adhesive-back business cards and folders.

One of Scott's cost-cutting measures was to plan for a large quantity, five thousand "of everything," which allowed him to pay only $1,700 for the entire system. Letterhead is important in Scott's self-promotion—he's found his greatest promotion success through first approaching the potential client with a letter. "I do research ahead of time, find out what their needs are, make sure there is a need for me, and then tailor a good letter to them." Scott states that due to his targeting of client needs and then addressing those specific

needs within his letter he achieves work with 90 percent of the firms he approaches that way.

Another economical move was to not print the envelopes and the folder; self-adhesive labels customize them with the Art of Business logo. Second sheets of stationery are used for business forms. Offset printed as "blanks" with only the name "the Art of Business" and no address, the second sheets are computer designed and laser printed for use as invoices, proposals and fax forms for each client.

Business cards were printed four-up on the bottom half of an adhesive-back sheet; two labels were printed on the top half. The sheet is split in half and the labels die-cut further so that they're ready to use. The four business cards are mounted onto a second color (teal) and then die-cut as well. Scott mounts the business cards himself. He selected this unusual method because the result is a card that is backed with an eye-catching color without two-sided printing and "it's hefty. It holds up in people's wallets." Before deciding on this two-layer card, Scott constructed a business card prototype and "carried it around for a month just

Letterhead System

Size:

Letterhead — 8 ½ × 11 inches; Envelopes — #10 and 9 × 12 inches; Folder — 8 ¾ × 11 ½ inches; Business cards — 2 × 3 ½ inches; Labels — varying sizes

Paper:

Masterpiece Granite DTP 24-pound Cobble Cream, Strathmore Grandee 80-pound Text Marina Teal, Masterpiece Environmental Woodstocks DTP 80-pound Cover Brown Bark

Type:

Garamond Condensed, Helvetica Black Condensed

Color:

Two match colors

Printing:

Sheetfed offset

Quantity:

5,000 of each (labels, business cards, folders, letterhead, second sheets, envelopes)

Total cost:

$1,700

Distribution:

Varies according to use

Mailing:

Varies

to make sure that it held up well.''

Scott's studio is in the basement of his home, but he uses an answering service and space in an office building as ''a base for client meetings and focus groups I assemble.'' The answering service permits his clients ''to talk directly with a human being and leave as extensive a message as they want.'' If Scott is available, the answering service forwards the call immediately to his studio or to any other number he chooses. Scott ultimately plans to locate his studio in the office building, which means he can use his current letterhead, imprinted with the office address, for a long time to come.

A World of Difference

Dana Lytle, Partner
Planet Design Company
Madison, Wisconsin

Graphic designers Dana Lytle and Kevin Wade met at a Madison, Wisconsin, advertising agency and destiny took it from there—almost immediately they started talking about setting up their own business. "We planned for about a year, established a strong philosophy about what we wanted to do, and jumped right in," Lytle states.

The partners' philosophy includes meeting in person with their clients, something they didn't get to do as staff designers; rejecting "formulas" and viewing each client as an individual with individual needs; striving to give each project a fresh approach; and not spoonfeeding the client's audience—giving them credit for their intelligence. "This business is not just about your design ability, it's also about the relationships you have with clients," Lytle notes. "It's all about communication. We try to present a unique point of view to clients, but one that's still right for their marketplace."

The firm's methods of obtaining its own low- or no-cost self-promotion materials are as varied as the clientele it services. Though in existence for only two years, Planet Design Company has already created its own low-cost flyer, collaborated with other companies to obtain samples that act as promotional tools to attract clients in new market areas it's approaching, traded services, capitalized on pro bono work, and developed a consistent program of press releases.

The first promotion piece the firm designed for itself is the "It's a Big World" flyer (pages 74 and

> *This business is ... all about communication. We try to present a unique point of view to clients, but one that's still right for their marketplace.*

75), created to introduce the new company to potential clients. Lytle states that in developing the piece, "we wanted to intrigue people enough to make them call us. We didn't want to give bios and pictures; we wanted a sense of mystery about us to get people interested." The theme of the flyer plays off the firm's name in both text and illustration and was distributed to the firm's entire mailing list.

The flyer, 9×22 inches when open, was offset printed on a 17×22-inch sheet; two letterheads were printed simultaneously in the remaining sheet space to give the firm a total of one thousand flyers and two thousand sheets of letterhead from the same press run. The printer did the printing for free, thanks to the relationship already developed when the designers were at the ad agency and the desire to work with Lytle and Wade in the future. Lytle estimates the unit cost for each flyer at approximately twenty-five cents. Paper cost $250 but also supplied letterhead for the firm; adding the expense of typesetting and miscellaneous supplies resulted in a total bill of "no more than five hundred dollars." Folded into fourths, the flyer was mailed first class without an envelope.

The response to the flyer was overwhelming: Within six months the two designers moved their studio out of Wade's apartment and hired additional staff. Since that time, the studio has moved again and two more staff members have been brought into the firm. Lytle notes that, even after two years, the company still receives phone calls from potential clients directly resulting from that flyer.

The firm's desire to break into two new market areas—the fashion and record industries—created a need for a specific, targeted promotion; collaboration with other firms proved to be the way to obtain an appropriate sample at no direct cost to the design firm.

The collaboration occurred between Planet De-

"In-Toto" Booklet
Size:
12 × 8¾ inches; 10 pages
Paper:
Cover — Buckskin 115-pound; Fly sheet — Strathmore Esprit Soft Blue 80-pound Text; Inside — Northwest Gloss 80-pound Text
Type:
Futura Heavy
Color:
Black, cyan, PMS 464
Printing:
Offset
Quantity:
Total — 5,000; studio received 250
Unit cost:
Approximately $1
Distribution:
Mailed and handed out
Mailing:
Varied

"It's a Big World" Flyer
Size:
Open — 9 × 22 inches;
Closed — 5½ × 9 inches
Paper:
French Paper Speckletone
Madero Beach 70-pound
Text
Type:
Six-line Block
Color:
Black and a special mix
Printing:
Offset
Quantity:
1,000
Unit cost:
Approximately 25 cents
Distribution:
Mailed
Mailing:
First class

BUT SOMEONE
H A S   T O
DESIGN IT

P L A N E T
D E S I G N
C O M P A N Y

THE WORLD IS A BIG PLACE, BUT
WE LIKE CHALLENGES. PLANET
DESIGN COMPANY IS AN ART &
DESIGN STUDIO THAT PRODUCES
EFFECTIVE GRAPHIC DESIGN THAT
AMAZES YOUR EYE AND ORBITS
YOUR MIND. 219 E. MIFFLIN ST. #3
MADISON, WI 53703 • 608.256.0000

sign Company, the clients—a modeling agency and clothier—the photographer, and the printer and resulted in a twenty-four-page, three-color booklet. Lytle and Wade provided the design, selected the photographs and did pagination at no direct charge to the clients, as did the photographer who took the photographs; the printer supplied the printing at cost. These services were provided in exchange for a portion of the finished product. The clients benefitted not only from the free services, but also ended up paying only about half of what normal printing expenses would have been for such an extensive project. Unit cost is estimated at one dollar.

A total of five thousand booklets were printed; Planet Design Company received about 250, "which gave us a substantial book that's directly related to fashion. It has a fun, hip feeling to it," which targets it appropriately to the interests of potential clients in the record industry as well. Lytle and Wade place the booklet in their portfolio when approaching these clients and use it also "as a direct mail piece. We send it with a letter that says, we'll call you soon to arrange a portfolio showing." The booklet is visual proof to these clients that Planet Design Company can create the type of work they're seeking and has brought several jobs to the firm.

In addition to these methods of obtaining promotional tools, trading services has also benefitted the design firm. Planet Design Company created a mailer for a photographer who, in trade, photographed finished projects for the studio's portfolio.

Pro bono work for nonprofit organizations in exchange for credit lines has also proven to be a valuable self-promotion vehicle. It creates the opportunity for the partners to "give something back" to the community while simultaneously increasing recognition of the studio's name through repeated public exposure. It has also earned publicity in trade magazines—the poster Lytle and Wade designed pro bono for the Madison AIDS Support Network was featured in *Communication Arts'* Exhibit section and *Graphis* poster annual.

Press releases are also frequently used by the studio as self-promotion that costs only the price of a first-class stamp. "We send out PR statements every time we get a new client or do something noteworthy," states Lytle. Whether published in a local paper, business publication or trade magazine, the publicity keeps the studio's name and accomplishments in the public eye.

More Is Better

Susan Greenstein
Illustrator
Brooklyn, New York

Susan Greenstein's illustrative style not only prints beautifully, but it also makes low-cost self-promotion a snap. Though it conveys the look of a woodcut, "the technique uses black gouache paint, which I draw on top of with a white pencil. Then I get a slightly overexposed stat made which eliminates any gray tones, so that I'm left with just black and white. If it's a color piece, I photocopy it onto watercolor paper and paint into it."

Specializing in editorial work, Greenstein has focused on illustration full-time for the past four years. She knows from experience that "self-promotion is extremely vital. Sometimes it gets difficult to be consistent about it because client work builds up, and you put self-promotion aside to meet deadlines. I try to send a promotion out once every two months. It's a lesson that I'm constantly learning—if you don't send things out it really does make a difference. You have to regularly remind art directors you're there because there is so much visual information coming at them left and right. Also when you're discouraged and things are going slow, that's really the best time to send things out because it raises your spirits. The minute you start working on something, you feel as if you're taking some action. You're creating this hope and the more you mail out, the greater the possibility that you'll get a positive response from someone."

Greenstein sends mailers to approximately two hundred people on a regular basis, although her mailing list consists of four hundred to five hundred names. The least expensive mailers are the black-and-white photocopies created easily through copy shops for under a hundred dollars. She pastes up type from a type book and stats it together with an illustration. When it comes to pho-tocopying "usually I'll paste up two or more illustrations on a page, have them copied and cut apart. I always put the mailers into an envelope with a cardboard stiffener. The cost is a little bit more but to me it's worth it because I want the presentation to be right." The cardboard and envelope not only make a more professional appearance, but increase the odds that the piece won't be damaged by the post office.

Illustrations that were originally printed in the *Cornell Alumni News* became the idea vehicle for Greenstein in the early stages of her career to show clients examples of her black-and-white work. She photocopied one thousand copies of the illustrations and turned them into small $4\frac{1}{4} \times 2\frac{3}{4}$-inch four-page booklets. Greenstein folded and stapled them herself, then mailed them out in an envelope. Her logo was stamped on the back of each booklet.

Having her logo made into a rubber stamp was another cost-cutting measure that Greenstein incorporated into her business. She uses it to identify her work and to personalize letterhead, envelopes, mailers and other promotional pieces. "I did the original design on scratchboard, made a stat, and had it made into a rubber stamp. It was something that was suggested to me early on and it helps to make information clear when there isn't copy on one of my pieces."

Although black-and-white samples are the least expensive of Greenstein's promotional efforts, she understands the importance of exposing art directors to her color work as well. "I do both color and black-and-white work and I want to emphasize that. So I vary what I send out. Art directors will see a black-and-white piece and not consider you for color work, so it's important that they see both" regularly.

Greenstein produces color samples on a Canon laser copier, which is "great if you're doing just a few pieces or, as in one of my mailings, you

Four-Page Booklet
Size:
Closed — 4¼ × 2¾ inches;
Open — 4¼ × 5½ inches
Paper:
White vellum
Type:
Custom
Color:
Black
Printing:
Photocopied
Quantity:
1,000
Unit cost:
5 cents
Distribution:
Mailed in an envelope
Mailing:
First class

Mailer With Mountains and
Bridge
Size:
3⅜ × 11 inches
Paper:
Uncoated cardstock
Type:
Publicity Gothic
Color:
Black
Printing:
Photocopier
Quantity:
500
Unit cost:
5 cents
Distribution:
Mailed in an envelope
Mailing:
First class

ILLUSTRATIONS BY
SUSAN GREENSTEIN

SUSAN GREENSTEIN 4915 SURF AVENUE, BROOKLYN, NEW YORK 11224 (718) 373-447

© 1991 Susan Greenstein

Maller With Fireworks
Size:
5 × 7⅜ Inches
Paper:
Uncoated card stock
Type:
Helvetica
Color:
Black
Printing:
Photocopier
Quantity:
1,000
Unit cost:
5 cents
Distribution:
Mailed in an envelope
Mailing:
First class

have an image that's small enough that you can paste up six on an eleven by seventeen-inch page. I cut them apart and then paste them onto cardstock to create my mailers. They ended up being only about one dollar a piece, but if you're laser copying a full-page illustration, it can cost three dollars per page. But there's a lot of flexibility with laser copying because you make only as many as you need." To prove her point, Greenstein cites her first promotional effort, a card that was offset printed; it portrays an example of her work that is very different from her current illustrative style. "Now I'm stuck with two thousand of

something that doesn't represent what I do," she explains.

Besides relying heavily on her mailers, Greenstein also advertises in a creative services book to keep her name visible. The book "is really helpful because its nature is different from mailing. First, it reaches prospective clients you wouldn't normally get to and it hits new potential markets. It's also good because it's on someone's desk without your mailing anything."

Keep the Client in Mind

**Supon Phornirunlit
Supon Design Group, Inc.
Washington, D.C.**

"I do not believe in doing self-promotion that doesn't mean anything. I don't want to make my self-promotion just another pretty piece because to me *that* doesn't mean anything." Supon Phornirunlit, founder of Supon Design Group, Inc., is true to his words having produced award-winning promotion pieces that are focused, have a purpose, and are created with a knowledge of the interests of the prospective client.

His attitude toward self-promotion formed early in his career. After earning his degree in advertising design, Phornirunlit spent evenings and weekends building his freelance client list while also working full-time as a staff designer. His first self-promotion piece responded to the difficulty potential clients had with his name. "I would call people to ask about freelance work and say, this is Supon, and everyone would say, what? They kept saying, what? What did you say your name is?" Instead of becoming angry over this obstacle, Supon turned it into an advantage, creating a promotion piece based on his name that could be sent to the client *before* he called.

The eight-page "misnomer" lists twelve ways his name has been misspelled, misused and otherwise abused in correspondence, including such priceless examples as Soup Phornit, Fupon Phornirunl and Su Porn. The result is a humorous yet informative brochure that greets you with a "Hello, My Name is Supon" name tag on the cover and lists his accomplishments and services opposite the chuckles. It accomplished its primary purpose. After re-

> *I don't want to make my self-promotion just another pretty piece because to me that doesn't mean anything.*

ceiving the brochure, "ninety-nine percent of the time the potential clients would remember me. They would say, oh yes, Supon, I got this funny promotion from you about your name. People hardly forgot my name after seeing that first promotion piece. You can turn things around to make people remember you, even if your name is very hard to remember. I think that's how promotion should work."

Freelancing became the financial source that let him buy equipment and keep his home-based business growing. Supon Design Group, Inc., formed in 1988, now boasts six members and a suite of offices. It remains a company that strives to be friendly and accessible, providing help and creative direction to clients, especially through education.

Meaningful self-promotion remains vital to the

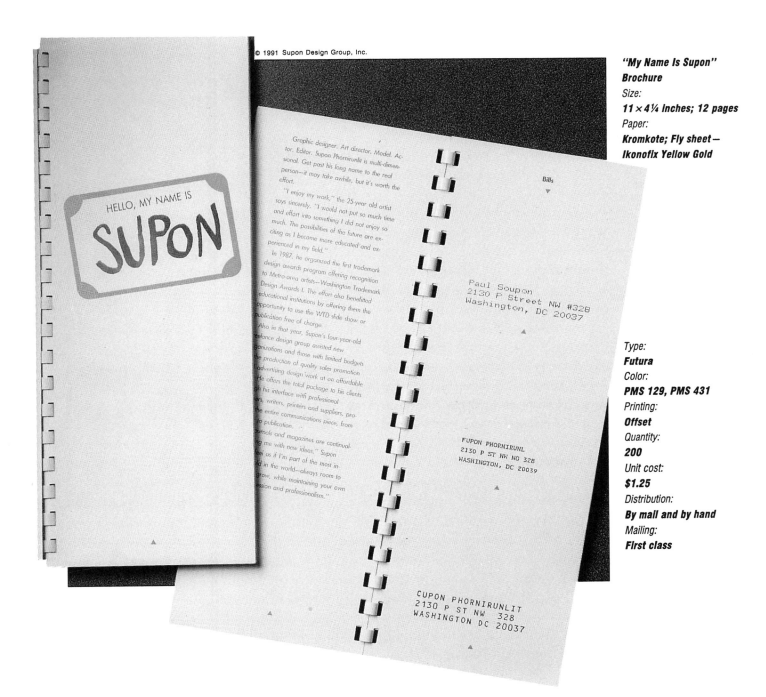

Graphic designer. Art director. Model. Actor. Editor. Supon Phornirunlit is multi-dimensional. Get past his long name to the real person—it may take awhile, but it's worth the effort.

"I enjoy my work," the 25-year old artist says sincerely. "I would not put so much time and effort into something I did not enjoy so much. The possibilities of the future are exciting as I become more educated and experienced in my field."

In 1987, he organized the first trademark design awards program offering recognition to Metro-area artists—Washington Trademark Design Awards I. The effort also benefitted educational institutions by offering them the opportunity to use the WTD slide show or publication free of charge.

Also in that year, Supon's four-year-old freelance design group assisted new organizations and those with limited budgets the production of quality sales promotion advertising design work at an affordable [...]. He offers the total package to his clients [...]gh his interface with professional [...]ers, writers, printers and suppliers, pro[...] the entire communications piece, from [...] to publication.

[...]ournals and magazines are continual[...]ng me with new ideas," Supon [...]eel as if I'm part of the most in[...]d in the world—always room to [...]grow, while maintaining your own [...]ession and professionalism."

Bills

Paul Soupon
2130 P Street NW #328
Washington, DC 20037

FUPON PHORNIRUNL
2130 P ST NW NO 328
WASHINGTON, DC 20039

CUPON PHORNIRUNLIT
2130 P ST NW 328
WASHINGTON DC 20037

"My Name Is Supon"
Brochure
Size:
11 × 4¼ inches; 12 pages
Paper:
Kromkote; Fly sheet—
Ikonofix Yellow Gold

Type:
Futura
Color:
PMS 129, PMS 431
Printing:
Offset
Quantity:
200
Unit cost:
$1.25
Distribution:
By mail and by hand
Mailing:
First class

growth of his business. "Doing a lot of self-promotion is the only way that it works for us," Phornirunlit states. Since "most of our clients don't have the time for us to call and chit-chat, self-promotion is the only way that we can contact the client. We usually do at least one piece every couple of months."

For Phornirunlit, self-promotion definitely is not a haphazard process. Each piece evolves with a specific purpose and goal. "The self-promotion piece itself shows people what you can do for them. I don't think that a good self-promotion product should show what you can do, but what you can contribute to your potential client. That's most important." Phornirunlit explains. "Think of a concept and package that tells people you're a designer. It doesn't have to look expensive, it just has to get the message across that you can do things for the client and you can do them well. You want the piece to speak for itself."

As well as possessing a purpose, pieces usually are targeted to a specific clientele, planned with a theme, and mailed on a timed schedule. Phornirunlit explains that "you need to treat a self-promotion as a project in the studio and not as just something to do because business is slow. I have self-promotion planned for each year. I target specifically what types of new clients or projects I want. Study each type of client, because if you don't, you might send something inappropriate and your self-promotion will kill your business, not promote it."

The firm mails approximately five hundred pieces out with each mailing, unless its targeted to a specific clientele, and often mails to vendors as well as potential clients. "Most of our promotions are cheap or easy to produce. A good promotion should sell your client on its concept," not its expense.

One example of a targeted, inexpensive self-promotion is the Identity Portfolio, a six-page spi-ral-bound booklet of logos, which are a design specialty of Supon Design Group. The brochure, targeted to current clients, is planned for associations that hold yearly conventions or meetings. "We send it out in March or April when they're preparing to set the convention budget for the next year and are planning for a new convention logo." This piece "reminds them that we specialize in logos and trademarks." Each inside page presents one logo, the client name and his service; the pages are printed in black only at a quick printer. The cover features the firm's logo, which, though it appears to be three-color printing, is actually gray cover stock designed to appear three dimensional: the center stylized S is die-cut and situated over a solid yellow sheet of paper; the other two logo lines are printed in black. "We die-cut the cover ourselves by hand, and the paper was donated by a vendor," to reduce costs. Total per unit cost for printing and binding was just one dollar.

A holiday greeting exemplifies the staying power and repeat client contact Phornirunlit plans into his self-promotion. For the greeting shown on page 84, Phornirunlit notes that "we wanted to do something really different. We wanted a piece that a client could *use*. Not only use, but when they finished with it, would call us back and ask if they could have a refill. This way we can keep in contact with the client." The greeting became a folder of stationery, one set of letterhead and envelopes for each season of the year—summer, fall, winter and spring. Its title, "Season's Greetings," shows the group's penchant for wordplay. "We found it appropriate to give at Christmas, but because of the four seasons we can give this package to potential clients year-round." The group has found that at least every couple of months a client will call to ask for the letterhead for one of the seasons. During these contacts, Phornirunlit states, "we can ask, do you have anything for us?" The paper was

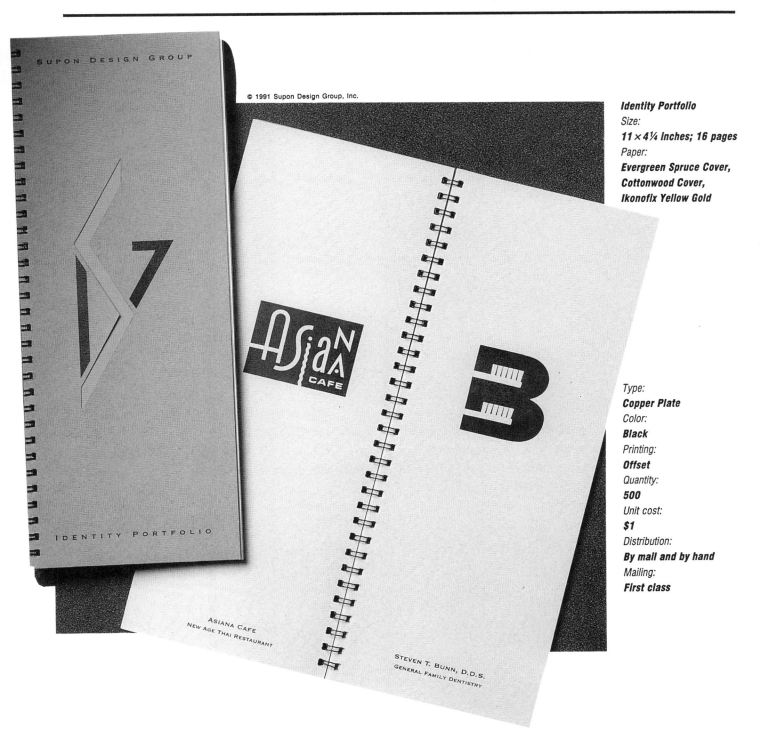

© 1991 Supon Design Group, Inc.

SUPON DESIGN GROUP

IDENTITY PORTFOLIO

ASIANA CAFE
NEW AGE THAI RESTAURANT

STEVEN T. BUNN, D.D.S.
GENERAL FAMILY DENTISTRY

Identity Portfolio
Size:
11 × 4¼ inches; 16 pages
Paper:
Evergreen Spruce Cover,
Cottonwood Cover,
Ikonofix Yellow Gold

Type:
Copper Plate
Color:
Black
Printing:
Offset
Quantity:
500
Unit cost:
$1
Distribution:
By mail and by hand
Mailing:
First class

"Season's Greetings"
Stationery and Folder
Size:
Folder — 7½ × 10¾ inches;
Stationery sheet —
7½ × 10½ inches
Paper:
Evergreen Text, Gainsboro
Script Wheat and Silver,
Protocol Writing Bright
White and Ivory
Type:
New Baskerville
Color:
Various (total of 11 PMS)
Printing:
Offset
Quantity:
500
Unit cost:
Folder — approximately $1;
Four seasons letterhead —
approximately $1 each
Distribution:
By mail and by hand
Mailing:
First class

Four Notepads With
Printing Terms on Covers
Size:
5½ × 8½ Inches
Paper:
Inside — Bright Water
(various colors); Cover —
French Paper Speckletone
Cover Chalk White
Type:
Text - Helvetica Condensed
Color:
PMS 485, Pantone Green,
PMS 301, PMS 165
Printing:
Offset
Quantity:
2,000 pads
Unit cost:
$1 per pad
Distribution:
By mail and by hand
Mailing:
First class

HOW

IDEAS & TECHNIQUES IN GRAPHIC DESIGN

$19.95

BUSINESS
ANNUAL 1990

WASHINGTON, D.C.

Supon Design Group, Inc.

In three short years SDG has enjoyed phenomenal growth and at the same time helped dispel the staid images of many D.C.-based businesses.

By Linda Klinger

In 1944, a somewhat perceptive man named George S. Patton wrote in a letter to his son: "Take calculated risks. This is quite different from being rash." No doubt Supon Phornirunlit would agree with him.

It took only 18 months and four address changes to propel Phornirunlit from a one-bedroom apartment/studio to the seven-suite headquarters of Supon Design Group, Inc., now situated in Washington, D.C.'s major business district. He quit his $29,000-a-year graphics job to bill an extraordinary $100,000 during SDG's first year.

"Our second year, we estimated $250,000 and actually billed for $320,000," the 28-year-old designer laughs. "This year, we project half a million, and we'll probably make it!"

In person, Phornirunlit speaks with a quiet intensity. But underneath the easy smile, the black hair in an updated, semi-short style, there's a limitless supply of good instinct. Though he appears to have lived a charmed life, he attributes his success to

level-headed business sense and inevitable hard work.

"People say to me, 'You're lucky, you've accomplished so much!'" he notes. "They don't understand you have to earn success."

A native of Thailand who has worked as both an actor and a model, Phornirunlit rests a little easier these days, as SDG has become a recognizable name in many parts of the Washington business community. Some of that esteem comes from numerous design awards that cover the walls of his expansive studio, where every office has a window, and pastel furnishings give the illusion of even greater

space. Since its inception, SDG has earned 31 awards including the Type Directors Club, *Print* Regional Design Award and Addy Awards, and has been recognized for his outstanding work in competitions sponsored by such organizations as the Art Directors Club of Metropolitan Washington, American Corporate Identity, DESI and New York Art Directors Club. Samples of SDG's work were exhibited recently in an international show at Jerusalem's Israel Museum.

"I've never wasted time working at anything I didn't like," Phornirunlit asserts. "People said I was too young to open a

business, but I felt that I could do it if I tried my best. If I failed, the worst that would happen is I'd go back to being an employee somewhere else."

Phornirunlit's philosophy was influenced by his father, an optician who loved to draw. His father encouraged him to seek art experience abroad, so Phornirunlit studied in Japan and the United States to earn his BFA degree in advertising design. But, after seven years in design, he maintains that schooling is a secondary factor in business success.

"It's mainly a positive attitude," he claims. "It's accepting support and encouragement from friends, and letting it fuel your motivation. And, once you grow beyond a one-man shop, it's teamwork. You also have to be a good businessperson as much as a good designer."

The primary strength of SDG is its ability to rise above the "stuffy" demeanor characterizing most of its competition. "Our clients tell us they prefer working with us because we're friendly," he relates. "Treating them like friends includes being honest. We don't want to

At the Jefferson Memorial are Supon Design Group, Inc. (left to right): marketing manager Wayne Kurie; designer Andy Dolan; art director/owner Supon Phornirunlit; production coordinator Jeanne Ristig and designer Dianne Cook.

Supon Phornirunlit sits in front of many of the awards his design firm has earned.

'Treating them (clients) like friends includes being honest. We don't want to be 'corporate'—we want to be accessible.'

A feature in a national magazine was turned into a self-promotion piece for distribution to clients during design presentations.

sold to the design firm at cost and, though the printer scored the folder, the group hand-folded and glued the folder to save money.

Another successful self-promotion, the four notepads, shown on page 85, not only provide a smile, but contribute to Phornirunlit's goal of educating clients. Each notepad's cover defines and illustrates a common printing term, such as color key; the accompanying visuals humorously convey the term in layperson's language. "We try to educate our clients because, most of the time, people who buy printing don't know anything about printing terms. Every couple of months we give a different pad away. The pads are fun and useful for the client. I wouldn't do a notepad that just says Supon Design Group and has our logo at the top. That doesn't mean anything to me; it's just another notepad. I don't want ours to look like just another self-promotion." The cover is the only part of the notepad that is printed. The paper was purchased at cost from a merchant and the group hand-glued the covers to the pads themselves.

Each finished pad costs one dollar.

Publicity is another self-promotion tool that Phornirunlit uses to his advantage. An article on his studio and work that appeared in *HOW* magazine's 1990 Business Annual has proven a valuable resource to obtain new clients. "We purchased reprints of the article and send them out as promotions." Current clients often only glance through the article "because they already know us," but the reprint is definitely effective with potential clients. "It impresses them that we were one of the featured studios," and when the firm shows it during its presentation to the client, "most likely we will get the account."

Precious Promotions

Lynn Tanaka
Tanaka Graphics
Minneapolis, Minnesota

Lynn Tanaka identifies completely with her "mascot" logo—a fierce-looking bulldog—because "that's how I feel about being in business for myself. You have to be a bulldog. He's kind of forceful and out there, and always persevering. One of my teachers at Parsons School of Design gave us five words to live by: perseverance, dedication, no compromise and patience. I have them framed over my desk so at three o'clock in the morning I can look up and get motivated. You really have to plug away all the time."

A 1984 graduate of Parsons in New York, Tanaka worked as a graphic designer in New York for a couple of years and learned the hard way that "about 90 percent" of an art career "is marketing yourself and the business end of the field." Three years ago she moved to Minneapolis and decided to seriously pursue her illustration. "A lot of times I'll get an art director who wants me to work on a logo identity and I'll do the graphic illustration and work the type as well. I don't like pure graphic design,

> **My whole theory on promos is . . . to make them so precious no one will throw them into a file.**

but if it's in conjunction with my illustration, I can do that." Her clients include editorial, advertising agencies and design firms.

Tanaka's self-promotion philosophy doesn't include routine mailers because she didn't get sufficient response from the "typical postcard. My whole theory on promos is to make them look a bit more hand assembled, and to make them so precious no one will throw them into a file. I want them to be so different that no one will throw them away. I love to go into clients' offices and see them sitting around or displayed nicely. I may not do a lot of promos each year, but I think the more special they are, the greater the impact."

Her most recent promotional effort is "Lynn Tanaka's Iconofolio," a $3 \times 3\frac{3}{4}$-inch gatefold piece that contains six icons offset printed in green on French Paper Speckletone Cream Text, a recycled paper. The text beneath the icons reads, "I think, therefore icon." The last page contains Tanaka's name and phone number. Each end of the gatefold is hand glued by Tanaka to the covers, black Letramax board covered front and back with coordinated paper. This allows the cover to match the inside gatefold, but permits a black cross section to remain visible. The metal Egyptian icon adorning the front cover is actually a charm Tanaka found at a fabric store, sold three to a package. She contacted the manufacturer in Texas and ordered a large quantity. As she constructs the iconofolios, she removes the ring from the charm and glues the icon to the front. The piece is held closed by a hand assembled strap of paper, pinked on the edges, glued into a ring, and slipped over the folio.

The development of the iconofolio was "inspired by a job I did with a design firm. Its client was a law firm, and the job was an announcement for which I did these little spot drawings. They came out so well, and the firm and client were so happy with them, I decided to do a promotion for spot drawings. Before this, I had never thought about promoting nice, well-designed spots; I usually think more of full-color illustrations." The response has been excellent. "I've gotten a lot of jobs from it." Tanaka had enough pieces printed to construct five hundred iconofolios, 250 for herself and 250 for her rep in Texas. Her cost for each folio is fifty-three cents.

To mail the iconofolio, Tanaka buys sheets of corrugated cardboard, stamps them with her bulldog rubber stamp, and cuts them into $4 \times 4\frac{1}{2}$-inch pieces. Two pieces, front and back, are taped

© 1991 Tanaka

Iconofolio
Size:
3 × 3¾ inches
Paper:
**Cover — Letramax board
and French Paper
Speckletone Cream Text;
Inside — French Paper
Speckletone Cream Text**
Type: **Custom**
Color: **Green**
Printing: **Offset**
Quantity: **500**
Unit cost: **53 cents**
Distribution: **Mailed**
Mailing: **First class; postage
52 cents**

Mini-book
Size:
3¼ × 3¼ inches
Paper:
Cover — Letramax board
Type:
Custom
Color:
Varied
Printing:
Laser copier
Quantity:
500
Unit cost:
$1
Distribution:
Mailed and handed out
Mailing:
**First class; postage 52
cents**

around the iconofolio and an address label added to one side. Each costs fifty-two cents to mail, a fact that Tanaka notes "means I can use only one stamp. With the cardboard on the outside, it makes a fast mailing piece."

A previous promotion, "Lynn Tanaka's Mini-book" (page 90), incorporates striking color, while remaining handmade and tactile, as Tanaka likes it. The 3¼-inch square book is constructed entirely of black Letramax paper that gives the book a substantial feel and makes it capable of withstanding wear. "I score the edge with an X-Acto knife and make the book by gluing the pages together and folding them." Ten illustrations as well as titles and a name-and-address illustration at the back are all color copies. "I have all the images color copied, then I cut them out and wax them down. I was amazed at how well the images turned out because the original illustrations are just colored with Prisma colors. I asked the copier operator to bump up the color." In the final mini-book, "the color just sings. I was really happy with it." Gold grosgrain ribbon is glued inside the front and back covers to give that extra personal touch of color and to tie the book closed if desired. The cost of the mini-book ran approximately one dollar

each, primarily due to the cost of color copying. "I butted up enough images on an eleven by seventeen-inch sheet of paper to get two mini-books" and produced a total of about five hundred.

Tanaka uses the mini-books "for out-of-town clients when I don't want to send my portfolio. It shows good examples of my work. I also use it as a thank you to people who have hired me and sometimes as an incentive, in the sense that I tell a potential client they can keep the mini-book if they use me." Mailed between cardboard sheets like the iconofolio, the mini-book's postage is also fifty-two cents.

Tanaka's letterhead system follows through with her desire for hands-on assembly and use of recycled paper. Offset printing in one-color on French Speckletone Oatmeal kept the cost for a run of one thousand each of letterhead, business cards and labels at approximately two hundred dollars including the paper, which was purchased wholesale. Tanaka makes her envelopes by hand fifty at a time and customizes them by hand gluing the label and return address card herself. Pinking shears provide the spiky edges on both the letterhead and envelopes.

© 1991 Tanaka

Letterhead, Envelopes, Business Cards, Labels
Size:
**All approximate.
Letterhead—8¼×10¾
inches; Business card—
2¼×3¾ inches;
Envelope—4¾×9¾
inches; Labels—varied**
Paper:
**French Paper Speckletone
Oatmeal**
Type:
Custom
Color:
Green
Printing:
Offset
Quantity:
**Letterhead, business
cards, labels—1,000 each**
Unit cost:
6 cents

Savvy, Serious and Fun

Collette Murphy
Collette Murphy Design
San Diego, California

Collette Murphy takes her design business very seriously—and does so with a sense of humor.

The serious side of Murphy revolves around meeting clients' needs with excellent design and in operating her business. When she started her independent studio two years ago, Murphy quickly learned that "not only was I a graphic designer, but I also had to be a very stern boss," a role that was new to her. Though she doesn't have full-time employees, Murphy hires freelancers during extremely busy times. She found that San Diego's "beach, fun and no responsibility" attitude held by some freelancers didn't mesh with what she defined as appropriate business behavior. "That part was frustrating. I started turning to friends, then, and asking for personal recommendations" for freelance help. Now "I'm very up front and I let them know that to work with me it's critical you be on time, you be here when you tell me you're going to be here, and if I lay it out that this is what my client is after, you pretty much have to stay inside those parameters."

Just as up front about her self-promotion, Murphy admits that she has not previously done any formal self-promotion noting that "I've been very fortunate to have gotten all of my clients through word-of-mouth, which is the very best kind of promotion. It's the lowest cost and the most credible."

That fact—the lack of prior self-promotion efforts—and the anticipation of clients' belt-tightening motivated Murphy to map out a marketing strategy. With a current client base consisting primarily of television stations and nonprofit organizations, Murphy decided to develop a three-part mail campaign directed specifically to a marketing field she wanted to work with more: creative directors in advertising, marketing and PR agencies. "I had enjoyed working with that group of people. They paid their bills on time, were the most professional, and had the most respect for what I was doing. So I targeted that area."

For this promotion campaign, she kept two main goals in mind: "It was really important to me to let people know a little bit about me, how my head works, and what my personality is. I wanted them to get the idea that I could make working on a project fun, but also that I was serious, and that was a hard thing to do." Her second parameter was that the promotion be low-cost. Though she wanted very much to do something visually extravagant with photography or illustration, she realized that "there are so many things I've seen come out that are visually wonderful, but they really don't give an idea of what the person is like."

To meet both of these goals, Murphy opted "to paint the picture with my own words," and developed mailers (pages 93-95) that contain only text and her logo. Murphy used copy she describes as "racy humor" in headlines to make recipients sit up and take notice. Straightforward text follows explaining each card's purpose.

In developing the mailers, Murphy was cognizant that risqué is sometimes risky. Her marketing savvy made her acutely aware that the humor wouldn't have been appropriate for some other market areas, but that with this targeted one "it worked." Murphy also was sensitive to the reality that what one person finds funny another person finds offensive, especially in the area of humor with sexual overtones. Murphy showed the comps for her cards to some of her professional business friends before going to print. "I said, okay, I'm really going to send these out. This is the last chance you have to talk me out of doing this." But they didn't talk her out of it; indeed, the friends thought they were "hilarious" and gave their approval.

Cost for the campaign was kept low by first do-

The best call-girl service.

Would you like to satisfy your deepest most creative desires?
Full realization is quite possibly only a phone call away.
After all, everybody needs a freelance design fix once in a
while. I may just be the girl of your dreams.
Whether you are looking for a brief encounter or a more
steady relationship to properly service your graphic needs,
Collette Murphy Design provides the best satisfaction.
Call to find out how.

Collette Murphy Design
2220 Fifth Avenue
San Diego, CA 92101
619/595-1445

Mailer
Size:
5½ × 8½ inches
Paper:
Dull Coat Coverstock
Type:
**Franklin Gothic Heavy,
Goudy Old Style**
Color:
**PMS 1655 Orange, PMS
432 Gray**
Printing:
Offset
Quantity:
**3,000 cards (1,000 of each
card)**
Unit cost:
8 cents
Distribution:
Mailed
Mailing:
First class pre-sort

ing a lot of research on production and then by applying cost-cutting measures. Each card is 5½ × 8½ inches, which allowed standard-size 8½ × 11-inch stock to be used with no waste. Also "it's two colors over one, which is very cost effective." The text is in a gray so dark that it appears black, and the logo in orange confirming Murphy's belief that "you can accomplish a lot with two-color and you can do a lot with four-color that says nothing. The message I feel is more important than all of the bells and whistles that come with it."

All of the cards' design and production was done by Murphy on her Macintosh computer.

Once copy was finalized, she output to a Linotronic imagesetter. She offered the project to several printers to bid on and the printer she used most often turned out to be lowest. Printing cost for a total of three thousand cards (one thousand per concept) was $137. Adding in the costs for the copywriting and film presented a total cost of $237 or about eight cents a piece.

Mailed out at one-month intervals—April, May and June—the cards' tremendous response pleases Murphy. Response from the first card, The Best Call-girl Service, was 5 percent, but is still eliciting response. "I even got a call about the very

Free peek shows daily.

Does seeing a little something in black leather arouse your interest? Act on your impulses, this is no time to be shy.

A bit of instant gratification is vital. So take an uninhibited look at the provocative portfolio of Collette Murphy Design.

Don't recklessly spend your quarters on the wrong show. Call, and we'll show you our book for free.

Collette Murphy Design
2220 Fifth Avenue
San Diego, CA 92101
619/595-1445

The second and third mailers in a series of three. See the illustration on page 93 for production information.

For cheap thrills call.

Are you trying to make a hot date? You have a need for something stimulating, but your funds are limited.

For most projects, quick deadlines come faster than big budgets. Seems like it always happens that way.

If it's been too long since your last good creative thrill, you need Collette Murphy Design for affordable satisfaction. Call for an attractive bottom line.

Collette Murphy Design
2220 Fifth Avenue
San Diego, CA 92101
619/595-1445

first card in July after it had filtered through the company. I sent it out in April, and I'm still hearing good things about it." The second card, Free Peek Shows Daily, had a 6½ percent response and the third card is already at a 2½ percent response. With a national average for direct mail estimated at only a 1 to 2 percent response rate, these cards are beating all anticipated returns. Mailing costs were also planned to be as low as possible. Instead of mailing first class, "I went through a mail house and sent them first-class presort, paying four cents per piece less than standard first class."

Murphy knew that the humor she chose was not going to appeal to everyone, but negative responses to date have numbered only two. There have been no calls whatsoever that indicate anyone misunderstood the cards' messages in spite of Murphy anticipating that "I would have to deal with some crackpot calls." Murphy admits she thought she might get more positive responses from men than women, "but it's about even, which I think says a lot about where women's heads are now."

With an obviously successful self-promotion effort under her belt, Murphy believes that her advice to others is primarily "just do it. Nike said it best." Treat yourself as a client. "Sit down and decide what you want to accomplish, who you want to respond and — do it. Be realistic. Decide how much money you can spend, find out how much it's going to cost to mail and what it's going to take to put it together, and then sit down and come up with something that fits those parameters. A lot of people I know have this pie-in-the-sky idea, then they're disappointed when they can only afford to do half of it. Their frustration makes them stop there.

"You are a client. It's important that you take yourself seriously. Just like you would fill out a strategy sheet for any other client or plan out a production schedule for a client, you need to do that for yourself. You have to take it just as seriously because if your self-promotion doesn't work for you, what have you done? You've done nothing."

> *You have to take it just as seriously (as your client work) because if your self-promotion doesn't work for you, what have you done? You've done nothing.*

A Wiz at Self-Promotion

**Susan Tyrrell, President/
Creative Director
Ruby Shoes Studio, Inc.
Watertown, Massachusetts**

If you believe in happy circumstance, you can point to the formation of Ruby Shoes Studio Inc. to bolster your belief. Before forming their own studio, Susan Tyrrell and partner Ed Hauben had been co-workers in an art department for a stationery/gift firm. Tyrrell was art director and Hauben head of art production when each individually decided to move on. "We kept running into each other at interviews," Tyrrell states laughing, "and finally decided that we had the whole shooting match between the two of us and started our own studio." Ruby Shoes Studio Inc. was formed in 1984. Business came in through previous contacts and referrals, and "before we knew it we had a small rented space, then moved into a larger space and now we have six employees besides the two of us."

The studio's name epitomizes the informal atmosphere and the type of projects the designers cater to and was selected despite friendly warnings that Tyrrell and Hauben were "taking a risk" with such a lighthearted company title. "Ruby Shoes was more of a fun name as opposed to just using our last names," Tyrrell explains. "We had designed children's products, had somewhat of a flamboyant background, and I had a thing for the Wizard of Oz, so we decided to capitalize on the aspect of doing fun projects." The name's selection was also affected by legalities—artwork pertaining to the Wizard of Oz is in the public domain, but Turner Broadcasting owns the rights to the movie, hence the name ruby shoes rather than ruby slippers.

Tyrrell and Hauben initially designed products for gift companies but eventually moved into the premium market. Their first big contract, when the studio was only two months old, was to do a "huge promotion" for J.C. Penney incorporating Sesame Street characters. The J.C. Penney project allowed them to work with Children's Television Workshop and to create a children's clothing club. This in turn led to working for premium companies developing clubs for toy manufacturers such as Hasbro, as well as designing the little toys that go into Cracker Jack boxes. Other projects and clients include packaging, health care and medical groups, museums, nonprofit organizations and retail firms.

Ruby Shoes' own self-promotion is often created with an eye to seizing the moment—piggybacking onto a client's press run is a primary means to keep down self-promotion costs. Never a presumptive process, piggybacking mandates that Tyrrell or Hauben checks with the client first. "When there is some room on the paper, we explain the available space to the client with the idea that *they* might want to use it for something else. A lot of times we've gotten them little postcards or small self-mailers or bookmarks, just to utilize some small area. But if they're not interested, we stop and consider if it's something we could use and then we ask their permission."

Self-promotion is always on Tyrrell's mind. When there's a lull in business activity, she brainstorms concepts and ideas and keeps them in a folder. "Then when a client's project comes up and there's room on a sheet of paper, I review my ideas to see if there is some way" the firm's promotion piece can piggyback onto the print run.

Energetic and cute, the Ruby Shoes Fan Club promotion pieces ideally portray the mind-set of the studio and were specifically targeted to ad agency art directors. Tyrrell points out that this is a valid marketing venture for the firm, because "a lot of ad agencies have art departments but we've been used quite frequently as consulting creative think tanks. They bring us in to generate flamboy-

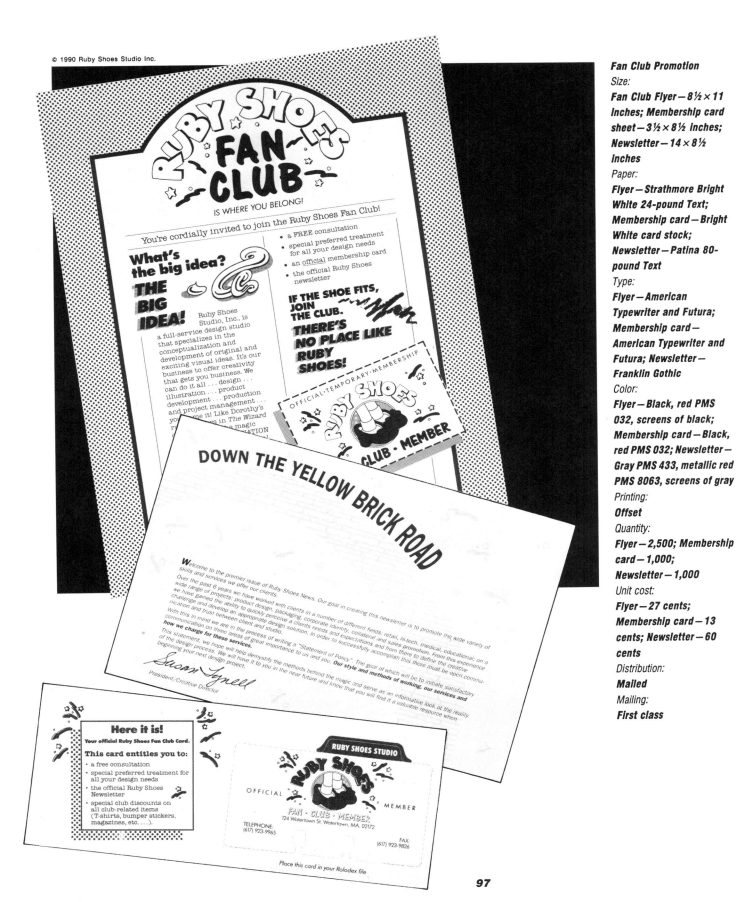

© 1990 Ruby Shoes Studio Inc.

Fan Club Promotion

Size:
Fan Club Flyer—8½×11 inches; Membership card sheet—3½×8½ inches; Newsletter—14×8½ inches

Paper:
Flyer—Strathmore Bright White 24-pound Text; Membership card—Bright White card stock; Newsletter—Patina 80-pound Text

Type:
Flyer—American Typewriter and Futura; Membership card—American Typewriter and Futura; Newsletter—Franklin Gothic

Color:
Flyer—Black, red PMS 032, screens of black; Membership card—Black, red PMS 032; Newsletter—Gray PMS 433, metallic red PMS 8063, screens of gray

Printing:
Offset

Quantity:
Flyer—2,500; Membership card—1,000; Newsletter—1,000

Unit cost:
Flyer—27 cents; Membership card—13 cents; Newsletter—60 cents

Distribution:
Mailed

Mailing:
First class

Mini-brochure and "Follow
the Yellow ..."
Frontispiece
Size:
**Mini-brochure — closed
4⅝ × 3¼ inches, open
4⅝ × 13 inches;
Frontispiece — 4⅝ × 3¼
inches**
Paper:
**Warren Lustro Dull 80-
pound Cover**
Type:
Isabel, Helvetica, Bookman
Color:
**Four-color process and
gloss varnish**
Printing:
Offset
Quantity:
5,000
Unit cost:
23 cents
Distribution:
Mailed and handed out
Mailing:
Usually first class

Follow the
yellow brick
road...

"Keep tight inside of them," said Glinda, advising Dorothy about the ruby slippers. "Their magic must be very powerful or (the Wicked Witch) wouldn't want them so badly.

Ruby Shoes Studio, Inc., is a full-service design studio that possesses a vivid imagination — just like Dorothy — and special talents — just like the ruby slippers. By putting our wits to work, we generate, organize, and coordinate concepts into attention-getting graphics and illustrations that spark interest and put your business name on the map — just like Oz!

Want magic in your message? Just ask. We can create excitement faster than you can say "There's no place like Ruby Shoes!"

We're also wizards! No matter your project, Ruby Shoes has the skills and knowledge to put you on the yellow brick road to success. With our excellent background in design, printing, production, market research, and art/illustration management, we offer a rainbow of experience — and impressive results.

Let us point you in the right direction!

"You're going to see a wizard?" the scarecrow asked Dorothy. "Do you think if I went with you this wizard would give me some brains?"

The tinman cared — and so does Ruby Shoes. Our concern for professional quality makes us do the utmost for our clients. Not only do we meet deadlines and follow through, we give maximum energy and effort so your company can achieve its heart's desire.

Are your creative abilities rusty — or just not there? Come to Ruby Shoes — we want to help!

"I'll see you reach the wizard," the tinman told Dorothy, "whether I get a heart or not."

"What makes the Hottentot so hot? What puts the ape in apricot? What have they got that I ain't got?" asked the cowardly lion. "Courage," his companions told him.

Ne**rv**e and nerve — that's what Ruby Shoes has in common with the cowardly lion! We're eager to try new techniques and technologies, and unafraid of breaking new ground. As leaders in our field, we welcome challenges and strive to be king of the hill — so you can be king of the forest!

Take advantage of our royal "red carpet" treatment!

50th Anniversary Flyer

Size:
8½ × 11 inches
Paper:
Strathmore Bright White Wove
Type:
Bodoni, Garamond, Eurostyle
Color:
PMS 032 Red
Printing:
Offset
Quantity:
2,500
Unit cost:
11 cents
Distribution:
Mailed
Mailing:
First class

ant thinking," especially when the ad agency is faced with a "fun" project it's not sure how to approach. Ruby Shoes is the ideal consultant "because we do a lot of promotional, children's and premium work."

The fan club promotion consists of an invitational flyer, membership card, newsletter and T-shirt. The flyer is a standard 8½ × 11-inch sheet printed in red and black, the ink colors for another job that was being printed "so we just bought more paper and paid the difference for producing the film and plates." The sheet features a "temporary" membership card with the offer to join the fan club. Membership includes a review of "our portfolio of award-winning work, a *free* consultation, special preferred treatment for all your design needs, an *official* membership card, and the official Ruby Shoes newsletter." The "official" membership card, printed on lightweight card stock, is presented to the creative director at the time of the portfolio review. Perforated to fit a Rolodex file, it has a bright red tab at the top to make finding Ruby Shoes Studio easy and quick. The Fan Club newsletter is mailed two months after a portfolio review and a Ruby Shoes Fan Club silkscreened T-shirt is a Christmas gift mailed as a campaign follow-through.

Tyrrell believes the promotion "stood out in the mail" because "a lot of people called us just to find out what we are." It also has won awards and been reproduced in trade magazines, such as *Print.*

Another piece, a full-color 3¼ × 4⅝-inch four-fold mini-brochure (page 98), has a client list on one side and Wizard of Oz characters on the other. Originally designed to be much larger, "the opportunity to fit the piece onto a sheet presented itself when we were creating an annual report for one of our clients," and the smaller version was produced. Actually, the *whole* piece didn't fit because of the page layout, so Tyrrell eliminated one brochure page and produced it separately on another sheet as the "Follow the Yellow Brick Road" piece. Ruby Shoes created all of the mechanicals; the filmwork and plates were added to the studio's cost.

The fiftieth anniversary of the Wizard of Oz, coincidently also Ruby Shoes' fifth anniversary, provided the studio with the opportunity to capitalize on its Oz tie-in. It generated its own products—silkscreened T-shirts and sweatshirts—which were marketed to the Wizard of Oz Fan Club mailing list through a one-color flyer. "We made enough profit to pay for the printing of some other things we wanted to do."

With a theme of "we hate waste," it's no surprise that Tyrrell advises designers to "look for economical ways to work with clients. One of the first questions we ask the printer is how he is going to lay out a job. A lot of people don't ask that question. Maybe he's buying an oversize sheet and sometimes there's a surprise in there—there's more room than you thought. Sometimes there's room to do some little shape that might be a filler in a mailer. Ask enough questions of your printer; I find that printers are a big help."

Promotion in Three Dimensions

**Stephanie Hooton and
Hien Nguyen, Partners
Pictogram Studio
Washington, D.C.**

In business as Pictogram Studio for two and a half years, partners Stephanie Hooton and Hien Nguyen agree that "one of the reasons we went into business for ourselves was so that we could pick and choose who to work for. If you can't do that, why work for yourself?" The firm has "a real variety of clients. We try to do a little bit of everything because it helps us to keep fresh. We have a cross section of clients—corporate, retail, the nonprofit sector." With this diversity in clientele, self-promotion campaigns must be designed to appeal to a variety of tastes.

When asked about a self-promotion budget, Hooton laughs as she says "as cheap as possible. That's our budget." Which isn't all bad if it forces you to be extremely creative and Hooton agrees that "that's the thing—it's the idea. That's always been at the core of what we do. We come up with a strong concept." Because she and Nguyen are both designers, "we do it together. We both have to like the concept and that's the only way we know if it might be any good."

One of the studio's promotion campaigns carries through a three-dimensional concept and is designed to keep the firm's name in front of clients with three separate mailings. The complete campaign consists of three red boxes, shown on pages 102 and 103, each containing an object that reinforces a message. Costing between $2.50 and $3 per unit including mailing envelope and postage, the boxes were not intended for mass mailings. When the idea was first conceived, initial mailings were to current clients and to select prospective clients as an introduction to the studio. Today, Hooton and Nguyen still mail the series out when they start working with a new client.

Each of the three boxes contains a different fold-out or participation mechanism. One box, featuring a miniature dart board and three small darts, challenges the recipient with the message that "Design firms always say that their ideas are on target. So, let them try to hit this from ten feet away. Or call us, we will be glad to show you how." Pictogram Studio's name and phone number follows.

A second box holds a miniature telephone and the text "Are you choosing a design firm for how big it is, or how big it makes you?" The kicker is "Don't you feel bigger already?" In the third box a fold-out ladder with a small bucket at the bottom graphically conveys the feeling of taking a risky plunge when deciding which design firm to use. The idea of eliminating this risk by choosing Pictogram Studio is reinforced by the message "If this reminds you of the act you have to perform when choosing a graphic design firm, call us instead."

Clever and fun to receive, the boxes didn't necessitate a great financial investment all at once. Because each is comprised of several components, the materials can be purchased on an as-needed basis, a tactic that permits costs to be spread out over a long time period. Only the printed text for each box was purchased in bulk with typesetting, paper and printing donated or purchased at a reduced cost from long-time vendors. The boxes were purchased one hundred at a time; the objects that went inside were at first bought "a few at a time." As the boxes proved to be a successful, continuing self-promotion device, materials were purchased in large quantities. All of the assembly for the boxes was done in-house by hand.

Sixty-five holiday greetings were produced in-house. Each consisted of a glass spice shaker nestled in a box (page 104). The spice shakers were filled with jingle bells. The card reads "Seasoned Greetings from Pictogram Studio." The shakers were purchased for $1.25 each and can

Box With Darts
Size:
5⅝ × 8⅛ × 1⅜ inches
Paper:
Hopper Cardigan
Cashmere 80-pound Cover
Type:
ITC Bookman Medium
Color:
Black
Printing:
Offset
Quantity:
500
Unit cost:
$1.70
Distribution:
Mailed in an envelope
Mailing:
First class; postage $1.50

Design firms always say that their ideas are on target. So, let them try to hit this from 10 feet away.

Or call us, we will be glad to show you how.

Pictogram Studio
202-483-4279

be used year-round. The greetings were both mailed and hand delivered. For shipping, each box was put inside a 5 × 5 × 5-inch corrugated cardboard box filled with hay; hand delivered boxes were wrapped in brown kraft paper or left unwrapped.

Though the partners don't use a set schedule for self-promotion because they like to surprise their clients with their pieces rather than having them expected, Nguyen points out that "you need to do promotion all of the time." Hooton expands on that with "the most important thing is to have a good portfolio, but self-promotion isn't just one

thing. It's a combination of everything — every time you talk to someone on the phone, when you go to see them, and when you actually give them a self-promotion object." Nguyen jumps in with the admonition to keep it "personal and entertaining" as Hooton adds that "it has to be really good. It can't be second best. You have to be extra picky. You are your own client, so you have no excuses for not having really good pieces. People look at it and that's what they judge you on."

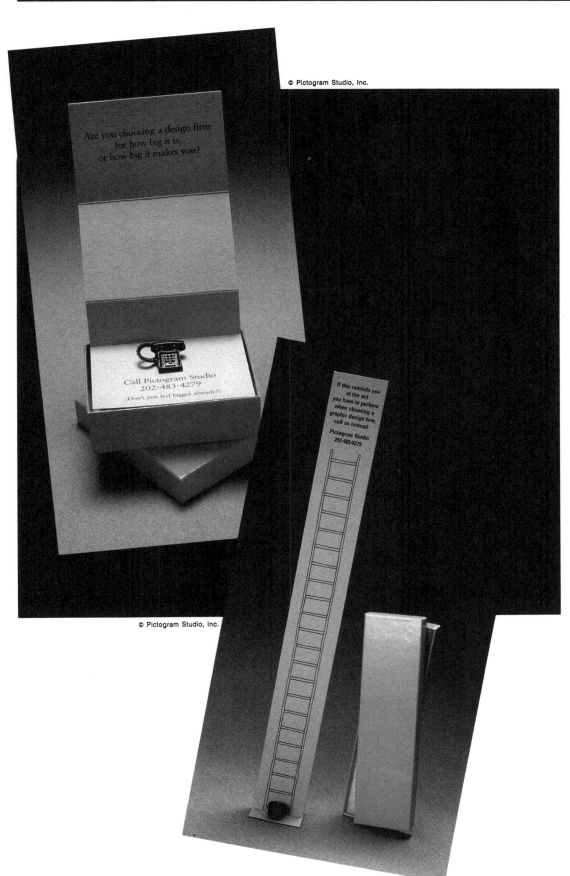

© Pictogram Studio, Inc.

© Pictogram Studio, Inc.

Box With Telephone
Size:
3¼ × 2¼ × 1⅛ Inches
Paper:
Hopper Cardigan
Cashmere 80-pound Cover
Type:
Bembo
Color:
Black
Printing:
Offset
Quantity:
500
Unit cost:
$1.50
Distribution:
Mailed in an envelope
Mailing:
First class; postage $1

Box With Ladder/Bucket
Size:
2¼ × 8⅓ × 1 Inches
Paper:
Hopper Cardigan
Cashmere 80-pound Cover
Type:
Univers 67 Bold Condensed
Color:
Black
Printing:
Offset
Quantity:
500
Unit cost:
$2
Distribution:
Mailed in an envelope
Mailing:
First class; postage $1.30

Holiday Box With Spice
Shaker
Size:
2 × 2 × 2 inches
Paper:
Label — French Paper
Speckletone Grenoble Gray
70-pound Text; Tag —
Champion Colorcast Dark
Green 8 point
Type:
Custom
Color:
Red
Printing:
Labels — photocopier;
Tags — by hand
Quantity:
65
Unit cost:
$2.36
Distribution:
Mailed and handed out
Mailing:
UPS; cost $1.25

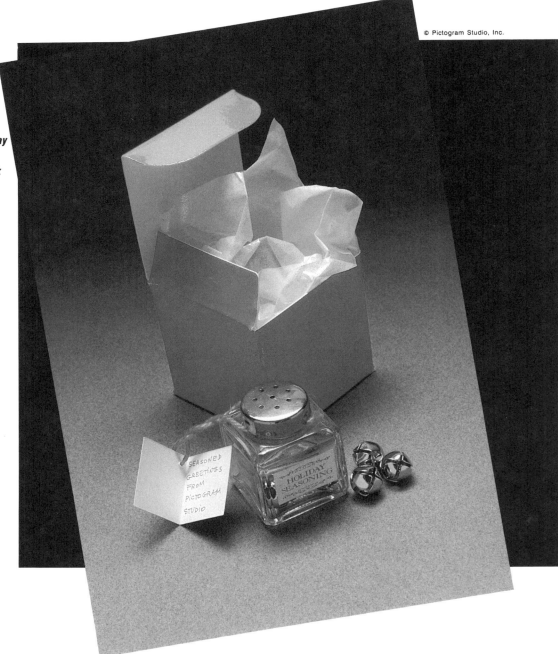

Promotion a Year at a Time

Shari Kura Smith
Shari Smith Design
Worthington, Ohio

Every graphic designer will encounter a learning experience, a project that, for better or worse, stretches creative and coping skills. For Shari Kura Smith, it was her own self-promotion campaign. Her complex and award-winning promotion began with an idea for a calendar. "One of my objectives was to create a unique item that would not only capture the receiver's attention but would remain as a constant reminder of Shari Smith Design. Since repeat advertising has a stronger impact than does a one-shot approach, I planned a three-month calendar (page 106) with four mailings, each containing a promotional letter with a specific focus."

Assistance from, and trade-offs with, a recently graduated art student, two illustrators and a writer helped the promotional calendars get off the ground. The new graduate provided a scaled mockup of the calendar, which was helpful to Smith because "I had not taken my idea to actual production" yet, and it gave Smith the opportunity to see how the graduate's thoughts developed. Two illustrator friends provided, for a nominal fee, some of the line art illustrations that Smith modified, scanned and traced with adaptations via the computer. A writer, met through a professional organization, bartered computer training for advertising copywriting.

Each of the calendars is die-cut and mailed flat, proportioned to fit into a 10×13-inch envelope that was specially designed for the promotion. The recipient folds the calendar into a pyramid, the panels held in place with glue strips. Rich with metallic color, each month contains a subtle background icon representative of the month: a heart for February, a kite for April, a football for September, for example. The icons are repeated in metal-

lic ink within the orchid purple border of the accompanying advertising sheet.

To achieve the precise look she desired, Smith worked closely with her printer. "Over the years, he has helped me with the tricky details of my more complex designs. I try to meet with him early in the design process so that I produce camera-ready art that works best to achieve the final results I want within my budget. On this piece I knew I wanted to use metallic inks and I knew that a currency cover metallic stock with rust ink overprinting would achieve the effect I desired for a much better price than printing with a metallic and a flat ink. I produced Cromatecs (rub-down PMS color matches) to check the chroma value of the orchid with the metallic and that proved invaluable in selecting the correct final ink shades." Enclosed with each calendar are the focused promotion letter and a purple instruction sheet that entices: The power of this pyramid will be yours. . . .

However, the project was not without its snafus, a situation defined by Smith as "an unexpected knot in the progress of a project. One of the things I neglected to do was to purchase a bulk mail permit and I paid dearly by having to rubber stamp that indicia on each envelope."

Then, "though I had produced die-cut, glue-flapped materials before, I didn't realize how high the costs were until I was paying the bill. To save a lot of money, I enlisted my family to apply glue strips to my calendars during the holiday vacation. Mistake! These things are not easy to apply. I tried three different tacks of tape and several applicators, none of which worked very well. Ultimately I bartered a brochure design with an illustrator to finish the tedious work of applying the strips. For those who haven't experienced the joys of this, let me tell you that lots of fresh X-Acto blades and rubber cement thinner are absolutely necessary. The glue tends to stick to everything!"

In spite of the obstacles, Smith acknowledges

**Calendar, Promotional
Sheet**

Size:
**Calendar — 9¾ × 12¾
inches, flat; Promotional
sheet — 8½ × 11 inches**
Paper:
**Calendar — 10 point
Currency Cover Metallic
Copper on White;
Promotional sheet —
Warren Lustro Dull 80-
pound Text**
Type:
**Calendar — Helvetica
Condensed Bold, Emigre
Modula, Helvetica Light;
Promotional sheet —
Helvetica**
Color:
**Calendar — PMS 499 Rust
(transparent ink);
Promotional sheet — PMS
8143 Metallic Orchid, PMS
8920 Metallic Bronze**
Printing:
Offset
Quantity:
**4,000 (1,000 each of
calendar, promotion sheet,
instruction sheet and
envelope)**
Unit cost:
**$2.50 per packet
(calendar, promotion
sheet, instruction sheet,
envelope and postage)**
Distribution:
Mailed
Mailing:
First class

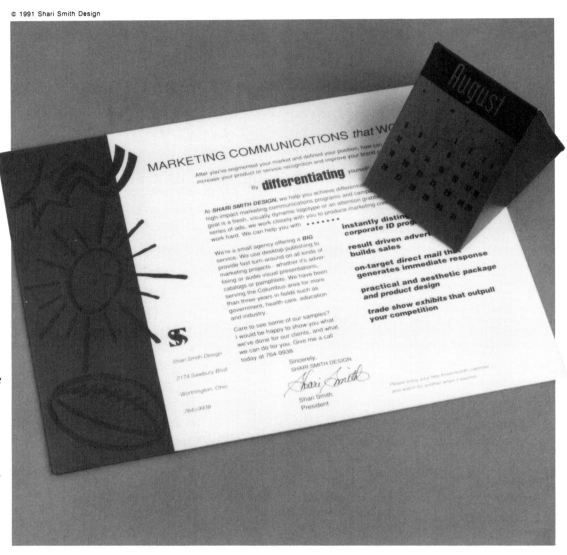

that "when the accolades started coming in, it was easy to forget the aggravations and even now I am hot and heavy into my next version of the perfect self-promotion calendar. Needless to say, there will be *no* glue strips this time. I am planning to spend about two thousand five hundred dollars, including mailing costs, which is about what I spent the last time. Since my mailing list was approximately two hundred fifty names, that works out to about a ten-dollar investment in each potential new client, certainly an amount that's easily recouped in one or two projects. I have received phone calls, compliments and awards of excellence for the calendars. They have gotten me in the door where I otherwise would not have had the opportunity to show my work. New business has been developing regularly as a direct result of this campaign."

Smith is keenly aware of "the importance and far-reaching effects of graphics in our society as a whole" and is a past president of the Columbus Society of Communicating Arts. Although she had explored her art options in the 1960s, Smith didn't discover the graphic design field until the mid-1970s and her interest "increased dramatically as

I studied letterforms, color relationships and two-dimensional design at the Columbus College of Art and Design." An entry level position gave her the opportunity to learn about advertising, direct mail, point-of-purchase displays, four-color process printing, slide presentations and photography. Then Smith "logged in four years as a graphic designer with a large corporation, two and a half years as an art director with a printing and exhibit/display company and one year with a Fortune 500 company." Even with that accumulated experience, running her own business is different. "As a sole proprietor I am uniquely aware of the big picture. Profit and loss statements are a very important aspect of my business. I am a designer, art director, sales representative and accountant. All hats must be worn and juggled so that the net profit is just that, *profit.*"

Memorable Mailers

Victoria A. Vandeventer
Victoria A. Vandeventer Graphic Design
Monterey, California

Designer Vicki Vandeventer believes in continuous self-promotion and so designed her year-long mail campaign to get her name in front of clients' eyes every few months. "I think it's important that you make your first big splash and then hit your clients again to remind them you're there. There are a lot of talented people out there" and continuous self-promotion means you won't be forgotten.

Vandeventer's promotion campaign consists of six mailers — three foldovers (pages 109-111) and three postcards (page 112) — one mailed every other month. Costs were kept down by printing only in black ink, offset printing all pieces simultaneously and by having the printer use paper, rather than metal, plates on the press. Vandeventer points out that "for short runs, they're really cheap."

As a freelance book designer specializing in textbooks, Vandeventer had two reasons for keeping her promotion low cost: One, she didn't have a lot of money to spend; and two, "I didn't want to look expensive. Particularly in college textbooks, if you look real slick and expensive, publishers won't call you because they think they can't afford you. So I wanted to go with a clever idea produced inexpensively just to show I could do that."

All of the pieces rely primarily on text and grab attention through wordplay and humor. Each of the 5½ × 11-inch foldovers serves a different purpose. Vandeventer began the mailings with the "You can hire me free (lance)" foldover letting it act as an introductory piece that Vandeventer followed up with a phone call and a personal review of her portfolio. Another foldover is a compilation of mailing labels received by Vandeventer that show how her name has been misspelled. She started saving the labels when she was senior designer at Brooks/Cole Publishing Company. "I received tons of mail there, so I stuck the labels in a folder and saved them for years." Seeing the name misspelled so many times compels the recipient to look to the bottom of the piece to note the correct spelling, exactly what Vandeventer wanted the piece to accomplish. "It is an unusual last name, so I do get remembered because of it," Vandeventer notes. The third foldover counts down from ten to two on the cover and inside states "Won" and lists the awards that Vandeventer has received.

The three 5½-inch square postcards each contain humorous one-liners and are "basically 'hi, I'm still freelancing,' " pieces according to Vandeventer. Mailed to publishers, design studios and ad agencies, the pieces repeat at the bottom the "You can hire me free (lance)" message of the introductory piece followed by Vandeventer's name, address and phone number. All were mailed without envelopes; the foldovers were held closed with self-adhesive circles.

Produced on blue, red, lavender and yellow papers, 150 copies of each of the six mailers were printed at the same time as Vandeventer's résumé and reference sheet for under two hundred dollars. The cost for typesetting was ninety dollars.

Seeking a new direction for her career prompted Vandeventer to compile and print her résumé with her mailers. Since 1980 she had been in book design, enjoying seven years at a publishing company and then five years as a freelancer where her primary clientele was publishers. Though she was getting "a lot of book projects, I was tired of that particular market. I wanted to expand into other areas, which is almost impossible if you don't have a background in them already. So I felt the easiest thing was to get a job in a related area."

To launch her job search, Vandeventer had two

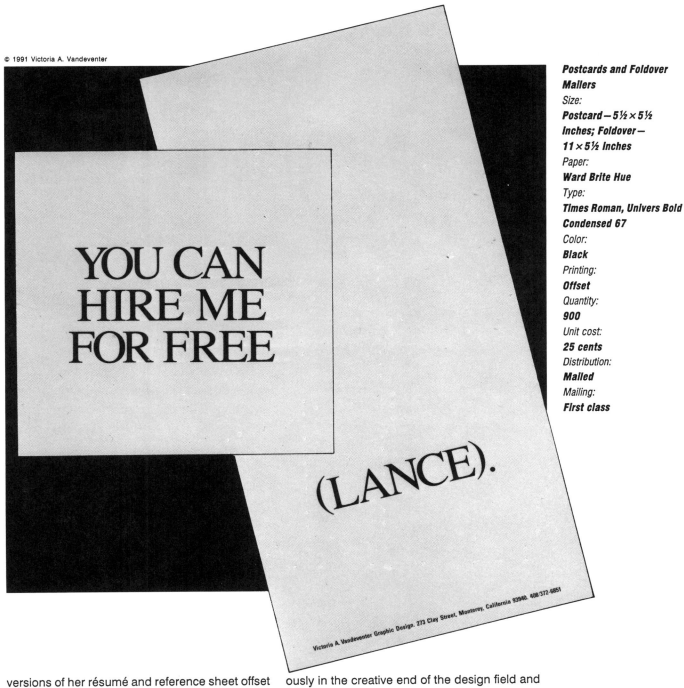

YOU CAN
HIRE ME
FOR FREE

(LANCE).

Victoria A. Vandeventer Graphic Design, 273 Clay Street, Monterey, California 93940, 408/372-6851

Postcards and Foldover
Mailers
Size:
Postcard — 5½ × 5½
Inches; Foldover —
11 × 5½ Inches
Paper:
Ward Brite Hue
Type:
Times Roman, Univers Bold
Condensed 67
Color:
Black
Printing:
Offset
Quantity:
900
Unit cost:
25 cents
Distribution:
Mailed
Mailing:
First class

versions of her résumé and reference sheet offset printed on silver Gainsboro 70-pound text: One set contained only type with the "me" from the word résumé set in large type as a dominant design element. On the reference sheet, *only* the "me" is printed. The other version of the two sheets contains a clip art illustration of a Reubenesque naked lady lounging behind the large "me." Her reason for producing the two versions was that "book designers aren't taken all that seri-

ously in the creative end of the design field and there's a reason for that. Books are supposed to be very comfortable and familiar and the design is not supposed to call attention to itself." But Vandeventer was now trying to reach a different market so she did want to display creativity and create design that called attention to itself. "I was afraid if I approached potential employers as a book designer they might think, she can only do boring old books. So the lady was to make the statement:

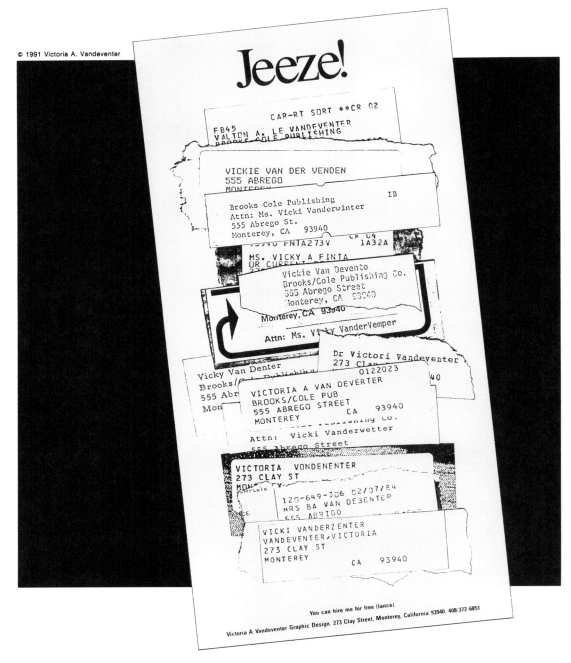

Not necessarily! It was supposed to get their attention so I could get in the door and show them the rest of my work."

But she used common sense when sending the "naked lady" résumé. "If I knew the people, the kind of work they did, and thought they would appreciate it, I sent the lady. If it was a company I was unfamiliar with and thought it might offend them or they might take it the wrong way, then I'd send the plain one. Usually at the interview, if I'd sent the plain one, I'd show them the lady and they always liked it better. Some were disappointed I hadn't sent it in the first place. It got great response." Her job search, which Vandeventer says she approached "not very actively," took approximately one year. She is a staff art director at Computer Curriculum Corporation, a job that doesn't involve any book design, which makes her comfortable accepting freelance book design projects when time allows.

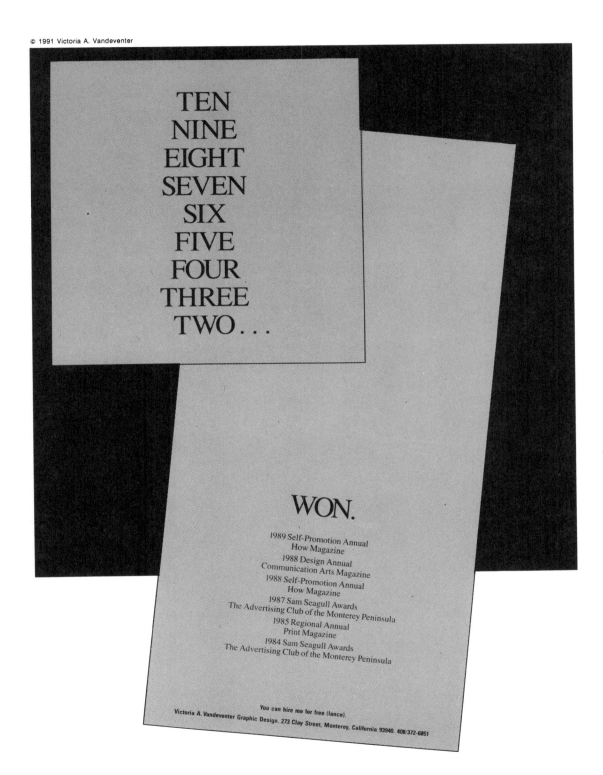

Résumé and Reference Sheet

Size:

8½ × 11 inches

Paper:

Gainsboro 70-pound Text Silver

Type:

ITC Garamond Light, Univers 67 Bold Condensed, Helvetica Bold

Color:

Black

Printing:

Offset

Quantity:

Résumé — 150; Reference sheet — 100

Unit cost:

25 cents

Distribution:

Mailed and handed out

Mailing:

First class

Permissions/Credits

All pieces used by permission. Credits are as follows:

Page 4
Moving Announcement
Illustrator and Designer: Michael Schwab
Printer: Julie Holcomb Printing

Page 5
Moving Announcement
Designer/Art Director/ Typographer: Gina Federico
Rubber Stamp Manufacturer: Mark-It, Springdale, Connecticut

Page 13
Art Director's Club of Atlanta Newsletter
Creative Director: David Levy
Designers: David Levy, Scott Mikus, Elizabeth Crawford
Illustrators: Scott Mikus, Elizabeth Crawford
Photographers: Dianna Thorington, Dennis Harkins
Writers: Dianna Thorington, Perry Mitchell, Alyson Storch, Linda Ure, David Turner, Penny Redfern, Cathy Barnard, David Levy

Page 17 (top)
Salt & Pepper Poster #1
Art Director: Rex Peteet
Designers: Rex Peteet, John Evans
Illustrator: John Evans

Page 17 (bottom)
Salt & Pepper Poster #2
Art Director/Designer/ Illustrator: Don Sibley
Photographer: J.W. Burkey

Page 18
Moving Announcement
Designer/Art Director/Creative Director: David Chiow

Page 19
Northwet Brochures
Art Director: Rick Eiber
Design: RED staff
Illustration/Calligraphy/ Photography:
Vol. 1, No. 1: Don Baker, Rick Eiber, Tom Draper, Jeff Boetcher

Vol. 1, No. 2: Rick Eiber, Chuck Reasoner
Vol. 2, No. 1: Rick Eiber, Bruce Hale, Ivan Chermayeff, John Fortune, W.T. Wiley, Rebecca Wild
Vol. 3, No. 1: Rick Eiber, RED staff, Philip Kovacevich, Kurt Palmquist, Ken Shafer

Pages 23, 24
Business Card Sheets and Letterhead
Designer: M. Brooks Greene

Page 27
"Over 25 Years" Mailer
Photographer: Jackie Dzuba
Paper: Barber Ellis Fine Papers
Printing: Paperworks Press Limited, Calgary

Page 28
As Happy As Larry! and Keen As Mustard! Mailers
Photographer: Geoff Yates
Paper: Barber Ellis Fine Papers
Printing: Paperworks Press Limited, Calgary

Page 30
Holiday Greeting
Paper: Barber Ellis Fine Papers
Printing: Merit Printing Ltd.

Page 32
Brochure
Designer/Illustrator: Robin Seaman
Copywriter: Rick Bursky

Page 35
Letterhead/Invoice and Business Card
Concept/Design: Karen Gourley Lehman

Page 37
Faux Snow Card
Designer: Jennifer Kennard
Production Assistant: Patrick Garland

Page 39
A R T Envelope
Designer: Jennifer Kennard

Page 41
Pyramid Promotion
Designers: Carmen P. Ramiréz, Roberto D. Colón, Laurel S. Rummel
Copywriter: Michael J. West

Page 43
Die-cut Portfolio
Designers: Carmen P. Ramiréz, Roberto D. Colón, Laurel S. Rummel
Copywriter: Michael J. West

Page 56
Moving/Expansion Announcement
Creative Director: David Levy
Designers: David Levy, Farrell Desselle
Copywriter: David Levy

Page 57
Holiday Card
Designer: David Levy
Photographer: Tommy Thompson
Copywriters: David Levy, Carol Levy

Page 59
1990 Box With Mistletoe
Concept: Kim Youngblood
Designer: Julie Sand

Page 61
Bag Mailer
Designer/Writer/Producer: Tom Graham

Page 63
Pop-up
Creative Director: Tom Graham
Illustrator: Linda Myers
Design and Construction: Tom Graham

Page 64
Maxi Harper Photograph
Photographer: Dennis Leach

Page 69
Christmas Card
Designer/Illustrator: Bob Upton

Page 70
Tom Scott Photograph
Photo: Courtesy of Andrew and Amy Cundil Photography

Page 71
Letterhead System
Creative Director: Tom Scott
Associate Designer: Elisa A. Ruhl

Page 73
"In-Toto" Booklet
Designers: Kevin Wade, Dana Lytle

Pages 74, 75
"It's a Big World" Flyer
Designers: Dana Lytle, Kevin Wade

Page 89
Iconofolio
Copywriter: Jonathan Skibbe

Pages 93, 94
Mailers
Concept/Designer/ Copywriter: Collette Murphy
Co-copywriter: Ed Castro

Pages 97-99
Fan Club Promotion, Mini-Brochure and "Follow the Yellow . . ." Frontispiece, and 50th Anniversary Flyer
Creative Director: Susan Tyrrell
Designers: Jane Lee, Lisa Smith

Pages 102-104
Box With Darts, Box With Telephone, andHoliday Box With Spice Shaker
Design: Pictogram Studio

Pages 109-112
Foldover Mailers and Postcards
Designer: Victoria A. Vendeventer
Typesetter: The Font Works
Printer: K/P Graphics

Improve your skills, learn a new technique, with these additional books from North Light

Graphics/Business of Art

Airbrushing the Human Form, by Andy Charlesworth $9.95 (cloth)

Artist's Friendly Legal Guide, by Floyd Conner, Peter Karlan, Jean Perwin & David M. Spatt $18.95 (paper)

Artist's Market: Where & How to Sell Your Graphic Art, (Annual Directory) $22.95 (cloth)

Basic Desktop Design & Layout, by Collier & Cotton $27.95 (cloth)

Basic Graphic Design & Paste-Up, by Jack Warren $14.95 (paper)

Business & Legal Forms for Graphic Designers, by Tad Crawford $15.95 (paper)

Business and Legal Forms for Illustrators, by Tad Crawford $15.95 (paper)

CLICK: The Brightest in Computer-Generated Design and Illustration, $39.95 (cloth)

COLORWORKS: The Designer's Ultimate Guide to Working with Color, by Dale Russell (5 in series) $24.95 ea.

Color Harmony: A Guide to Creative Color Combinations, by Hideaki Chijiiwa $15.95 (paper)

Complete Airbrush & Photoretouching Manual, by Peter Owen & John Sutcliffe $24.95 (cloth)

The Complete Book of Caricature, by Bob Staake $18.95

The Complete Guide to Greeting Card Design & Illustration, by Eva Szela $29.95 (cloth)

Creating Dynamic Roughs, by Alan Swann $12.95 (cloth)

Creative Director's Sourcebook, by Nick Souter & Stuart Newman $34.95 (cloth)

Design Rendering Techniques, by Dick Powell $29.95 (cloth)

Desktop Publisher's Easy Type Guide, by Don Dewsnap $19.95 (paper)

The Designer's Commonsense Business Book, by Barbara Ganim $22.95 (paper)

Designing with Color, by Roy Osborne $26.95 (cloth)

Dynamic Airbrush, by David Miller & James Effler $29.95 (cloth)

59 More Studio Secrets, by Susan Davis $12.95 (cloth)

47 Printing Headaches (and How to Avoid Them), by Linda S. Sanders $24.95 (paper)

Getting It Printed, by Beach, Shepro & Russon $29.50 (paper)

Getting Started as a Freelance Illustrator or Designer, by Michael Fleischman $16.95 (paper)

Getting the Max from Your Graphics Computer, by Lisa Walker & Steve Blount $27.95 (paper)

The Graphic Artist's Guide to Marketing & Self Promotion, by Sally Prince Davis $19.95 (paper)

The Graphic Designer's Basic Guide to the Macintosh, by Meyerowitz and Sanchez $19.95 (paper)

Graphic Design: New York, by D.K. Holland, Steve Heller & Michael Beirut $49.95 (cloth)

Graphic Idea Notebook, by Jan V. White $19.95 (paper)

Guild 7: The Architects Source, $27.95 (cloth)

Handbook of Pricing & Ethical Guidelines, 7th edition, by The Graphic Artist's Guild $22.95 (paper)

HOT AIR: An Explosive Collection of Top Airbrush Illustration $39.95 (cloth)

How'd They Design & Print That?, $26.95 (cloth)

How to Check and Correct Color Proofs, by David Bann $27.95 (cloth)

How to Design Trademarks & Logos, by Murphy & Rowe $19.95 (paper)

How to Draw & Sell Comic Strips, by Alan McKenzie $19.95 (cloth)

How to Find and Work with an Illustrator, by Martin Colyer $8.95 (cloth)

How to Get Great Type Out of Your Computer, by James Felici $22.95 (paper)

How to Make Your Design Business Profitable, by Joyce Stewart $21.95 (paper)

How to Understand & Use Design & Layout, by Alan Swann $21.95 (paper)

How to Understand & Use Grids, by Alan Swann $12.95

International Logotypes 2, edited by Yasaburo Kuwayama $24.95 (paper)

Label Design 3, by Walker and Blount $49.95 (cloth)

Labels & Tags Collection, $34.95 (paper)

Legal Guide for the Visual Artist, Revised Edition by Tad Crawford $8.95 (paper)

Licensing Art & Design, by Caryn Leland $12.95 (paper)

Make It Legal, by Lee Wilson $18.95 (paper)

Making a Good Layout, by Lori Siebert & Lisa Ballard $24.95 (cloth)

Making Your Computer a Design & Business Partner, by Walker and Blount $27.95 (paper)

Marker Rendering Techniques, by Dick Powell & Patricia Monahan $32.95 (cloth)

New & Notable Product Design, by Christie Thomas & the editors of *International Design* Magazine $49.95 (cloth)

Papers for Printing, by Mark Beach & Ken Russon $39.50 (paper)

Presentation Techniques for the Graphic Artist, by Jenny Mulherin $9.95 (cloth)

Primo Angeli: Designs for Marketing, $19.95 (paper)

Print's Best Corporate Publications $34.95 (cloth)

Print's Best Letterheads & Business Cards, $34.95 (cloth)

Print's Best Logos & Symbols 2, $34.95 (cloth)

The Best of Neon, Edited by Vilma Barr $59.95 (cloth)

The Professional Designer's Guide to Marketing Your Work, by Mary Yeung $29.95

3-D Illustration Awards Annual II, $59.95 (cloth)

Type & Color: A Handbook of Creative Combinations, by Cook and Fleury $39.95 (cloth)

Type: Design, Color, Character & Use, by Michael Beaumont $19.95 (paper)

Type in Place, by Richard Emery $34.95 (cloth)

Type Recipes, by Gregory Wolfe $19.95 (paper)

Typewise, written & designed by Kit Hinrichs with Delphine Hirasuna $39.95

The Ultimate Portfolio, by Martha Metzdorf $32.95

Art & Activity Books For Kids

Draw!, by Kim Solga $11.95

Paint!, by Kim Solga $11.95

Make Clothes Fun!, by Kim Solga $11.95

Make Prints!, by Kim Solga $11.95

Make Gifts!, by Kim Solga $11.95

Make Sculptures!, by Kim Solga $11.95

Watercolor

Basic Watercolor Techniques, edited by Greg Albert & Rachel Wolf $14.95 (paper)

Buildings in Watercolor, by Richard S. Taylor $24.95 (paper)

The Complete Watercolor Book, by Wendon Blake $29.95 (cloth)

Fill Your Watercolors with Light and Color, by Roland Roycraft $28.95 (cloth)

Flower Painting, by Paul Riley $27.95 (cloth)
How To Make Watercolor Work for You, by Frank Nofer $27.95 (cloth)
Jan Kunz Watercolor Techniques Workbook 1: Painting the Still Life, by Jan Kunz $12.95 (paper)
Jan Kunz Watercolor Techniques Workbook 2: Painting Children's Portraits, by Jan Kunz $12.95 (paper)
The New Spirit of Watercolor, by Mike Ward $21.95 (paper)
Painting Nature's Details in Watercolor, by Cathy Johnson $22.95 (paper)
Painting Watercolor Portraits That Glow, by Jan Kunz $27.95 (cloth)
Splash I, edited by Greg Albert & Rachel Wolf $29.95
Starting with Watercolor, by Rowland Hilder $12.50 (cloth)
Tony Couch Watercolor Techniques, by Tony Couch $14.95 (paper)
Watercolor Impressionists, edited by Ron Ranson $45.00 (cloth)
Watercolor Painter's Solution Book, by Angela Gair $19.95 (paper)
Watercolor Painter's Pocket Palette, edited by Moira Clinch $15.95 (cloth)
Watercolor: Painting Smart, by Al Stine $27.95 (cloth)
Watercolor Workbook: Zoltan Szabo Paints Landscapes, by Zoltan Szabo $13.95 (paper)
Watercolor Workbook: Zoltan Szabo Paints Nature, by Zoltan Szabo $13.95 (paper)
Watercolor Workbook, by Bud Biggs & Lois Marshall $22.95 (paper)
Watercolor: You Can Do It!, by Tony Couch $29.95 (cloth)
Webb on Watercolor, by Frank Webb $29.95 (cloth)
The Wilcox Guide to the Best Watercolor Paints, by Michael Wilcox $24.95 (paper)

Mixed Media

The Artist's Complete Health & Safety Guide, by Monona Rossol $16.95 (paper)
The Artist's Guide to Using Color, by Wendon Blake $27.95 (cloth)
Basic Drawing Techniques, edited by Greg Albert & Rachel Wolf $14.95 (paper)
Blue and Yellow Don't Make Green, by Michael Wilcox $24.95 (cloth)
Bodyworks: A Visual Guide to Drawing the Figure, by Marbury Hill Brown $24.95 (cloth)
Business & Legal Forms for Fine Artists, by Tad Crawford $4.95 (paper)
Capturing Light & Color with Pastel, by Doug Dawson $27.95 (cloth)
Colored Pencil Drawing Techniques, by Iain Hutton-Jamieson $24.95 (cloth)
The Complete Acrylic Painting Book, by Wendon Blake $29.95 (cloth)
The Complete Book of Silk Painting, by Diane Tuckman & Jan Janas $24.95 (cloth)
The Complete Colored Pencil Book, by Bernard Poulin $27.95 (cloth)
The Complete Guide to Screenprinting, by Brad Faine $24.95 (cloth)
The Creative Artist, by Nita Leland $27.95 (cloth)
Creative Basketmaking, by Lois Walpole $12.95 (cloth)
Creative Painting with Pastel, by Carole Katchen $27.95 (cloth)
Decorative Painting for Children's Rooms, by Rosie Fisher $10.50 (cloth)
The Dough Book, by Toni Bergli Joner $15.95 (cloth)
Drawing & Painting Animals, by Cecile Curtis $26.95 (cloth)
Exploring Color, by Nita Leland $24.95 (paper)
Festive Folding, by Paul Jackson $17.95 (cloth)
Fine Artist's Guide to Showing & Selling Your Work, by Sally Price Davis $17.95 (paper)
Getting Started in Drawing, by Wendon Blake $24.95
The Half Hour Painter, by Alwyn Crawshaw $19.95 (paper)
Handtinting Photographs, by Martin and Colbeck $29.95 (cloth)
How to Paint Living Portraits, by Roberta Carter Clark $27.95 (cloth)
How to Succeed As An Artist In Your Hometown, by Stewart P. Biehl $24.95 (paper)
Introduction to Batik, by Griffin & Holmes $9.95 (paper)
Keys to Drawing, by Bert Dodson $21.95 (paper)
Master Strokes, by Jennifer Bennell $27.95 (cloth)
The North Light Illustrated Book of Painting Techniques, by Elizabeth Tate $29.95 (cloth)
Oil Painting: Develop Your Natural Ability, by Charles Sovek $29.95
Painting Floral Still Lifes, by Joyce Pike $19.95 (paper)
Painting Flowers with Joyce Pike, by Joyce Pike $27.95 (cloth)
Painting Landscapes in Oils, by Mary Anna Goetz $27.95 (cloth)
Painting More Than the Eye Can See, by Robert Wade $29.95 (cloth)
Painting Seascapes in Sharp Focus, by Lin Seslar $22.95 (paper)
Painting the Beauty of Flowers with Oils, by Pat Moran $27.95 (cloth)
Pastel Painting Techniques, by Guy Roddon $19.95 (paper)
The Pencil, by Paul Calle $19.95 (paper)
Perspective Without Pain, by Phil Metzger $19.95 (paper)
Putting People in Your Paintings, by J. Everett Draper $19.95 (paper)
Realistic Figure Drawing, by Joseph Sheppard $19.95 (paper)
Tonal Values: How to See Them, How to Paint Them, by Angela Gair $19.95 (paper)

To order directly from the publisher, include $3.00 postage and handling for one book, $1.00 for each additional book. Allow 30 days for delivery.

North Light Books
1507 Dana Avenue, Cincinnati, Ohio 45207
Credit card orders call TOLL-FREE
1-800-289-0963
Prices subject to change without notice.